Thomas Cook

CITYSPOTS
BORDEAUX

WHAT'S IN YOUR GUIDEBOOK?

Independent authors Impartial up-to-date information from our travel experts who meticulously source local knowledge.

Experience Thomas Cook's 165 years in the travel industry and guidebook publishing enriches every word with expertise you can trust.

Travel know-how Contributions by thousands of staff around the globe, each one living and breathing travel.

Editors Travel-publishing professionals, pulling everything together to craft a perfect blend of words, pictures, maps and design.

You, the traveller We deliver a practical, no-nonsense approach to information, geared to how you really use it.

ABOUT THE AUTHOR

Jane Anson is a writer and columnist, based in Bordeaux, France and the author of Thomas Cook's HotSpot Corsica and CitySpot Toulouse guidebooks. She also writes widely for the *Telegraph*, the *Irish Independent*, *Food & Travel*, *Gourmet Traveller* and *Wine & Spirit* magazines, plus a number of other international publications.

CITYSPOTS
BORDEAUX

Jane Anson

Written by Jane Anson

Published by Thomas Cook Publishing
A division of Thomas Cook Tour Operations Limited
Company registration No: 1450464 England
The Thomas Cook Business Park, 9 Coningsby Road
Peterborough PE3 8SB, United Kingdom
Email: books@thomascook.com, Tel: +44 (0)1733 416477
www.thomascookpublishing.com

Produced by The Content Works Ltd
Aston Court, Kingsmead Business Park, Frederick Place
High Wycombe, Bucks HP11 1LA
www.thecontentworks.com

Series design based on an original concept by Studio 183 Limited

ISBN: 978-1-84157-943-6

First edition © 2008 Thomas Cook Publishing
Text © Thomas Cook Publishing
Maps © Thomas Cook Publishing/PCGraphics (UK) Limited
Transport map © Communicarta Limited

Series Editor: Kelly Anne Pipes
Project Editor: Linda Bass
Production/DTP: Steven Collins

Printed and bound in Spain by GraphyCems

Cover photography (Cathédrale Saint-André) © Andy Arthur/Alamy

CONTENTS

SYMBOLS KEY

The following symbols are used throughout this book:

ⓐ address ☏ telephone ⓕ fax ⓦ website address ⓔ email
🕐 opening times Ⓝ public transport connections

The following symbols are used on the maps:

🅸 information office		▨ points of interest
✈ airport		O city
➕ hospital		O large town
🛡 police station		○ small town
🚌 bus station		═ motorway
🚆 railway station		— main road
✝ cathedral		— minor road
❶ numbers denote		— railway
featured cafés & restaurants		

Hotels and restaurants are graded by approximate price as follows:
£ budget price ££ mid-range price £££ expensive

Abbreviations used in addresses:

av.   avenue
blvd boulevard
pl.   place (square)

▶ *The rooftop, spires and streets of Bordeaux*

INTRODUCING
Bordeaux

Introduction

Bordeaux is the epitome of an elegant French city, with its sweeping, 18th-century waterfront and tree-lined boulevards. Defined by its wine the world over, sometimes it has also been limited by it and written off as snooty and self-important, a verdict that any modern-day visitor would reject. Bordeaux has never been so ripe for a second look. Declared a UNESCO World Heritage Site in 2007, and with almost 350 buildings classified as historic monuments (the only French city to beat this number is Paris), Bordeaux has woken up to the fact that its cultural heritage extends far beyond the grape. It's still rightly known for the quality of its vineyards, of course, but the city is also turning into a culturally vibrant centre, with a sleek new tram system and spruced up quays lining either side of the Garonne River with parks, restaurants and bars.

Today's Bordeaux is also one of the high-tech centres of France, with 20,000 people employed in the aeronautical industry. Its position on the Atlantic coast, just a few hours from the Spanish border, makes its chic resorts increasingly attractive to growing numbers of visitors. The river banks of the Garonne, deep enough to welcome cruise ships right into the centre of the city, still see the arrival and departure of almost eight million tonnes (7.87 million tons) of goods each year, and the city centre boasts the longest pedestrianised shopping street in Europe. Bordeaux is a surprising city to visit in many ways. Put aside those out-of-date expectations, and a few days' exploration will show why UNESCO described the city as a 'melting pot of humanism, universality and culture'.

⬥ Just one of Bordeaux's numerous caves a vin (wine cellars)

When to go

Bordeaux offers something for visitors year round. In summer, you are only half an hour from the beaches of Arcachon and the Atlantic Coast, with its many surfing resorts, while in the city centre the Miroir d'Eau (see page 62) provides hours of splashing opportunities. In winter, there are the truffles of Périgord in the Dordogne region an hour to the east, plus the restaurants, theatre and Christmas market of the city centre.

SEASONS & CLIMATE

The city of Bordeaux is only 80 km (50 miles) inland from the Atlantic Ocean, on the Garonne River. The Gulf Stream passes right by, which means mild temperatures through most of the year, and few extremes. Average temperatures range from 10°–30°C (50°–86°F), with a few freezing periods in winter, and some days in summer when it may climb up to 40°C (104°F).

ANNUAL EVENTS

The events scene in Bordeaux is just getting better and better. Despite the inevitable focus on wine, the city is making increasingly louder bleeps on the radar of a wider cultural agenda.

January
Jumping International The Bordeaux region is known for its show-jumping events, and this is the largest of the year, held at

Bordeaux Lac in the first week of the month. ☎ (05) 56 11 99 00
🅦 www.bordeaux-expo.com/jumping 🅝 Bus: 31

May

Garden Festival All the city's parks open up and hold special
events all month, from dance and opera to children's theatre.
🅐 Hôtel de Ville (Bordeaux Town Hall), pl. Pey-Berland
☎ (05) 56 10 20 30

Union Grand Crus Wine Weekend For one weekend
(check website for dates), the region's top wine châteaux

🔺 *The Fête du Vin is Europe's largest wine festival*

hold tastings for the general public in central Bordeaux.
📍 Union des Grand Crus, 10 cours du 30 Juillet
📞 (05) 56 51 91 91 🌐 www.ugcb.net

June–Aug

Bordeaux Pride On the first Saturday in June, the gay pride
festival holds its Bordeaux bash, with a colourful procession
and party. 🌐 www.lgpbordeaux.net

Les Épicuriales Annual food festival held from the end of June
(and into July) in the allées de Tourny, with a variety of the
world's cuisines. 📞 (05) 56 00 66 00

Fête du Vin Europe's biggest wine festival, with each of the
producers setting up tasting stands around the place des
Quinconces and the river banks. 📞 (05) 56 00 66 00
🌐 www.bordeaux-fete-le-vin.com

Les Estivales du Musique (Summer Music) Various classical
concerts take place all summer in châteaux around the Médoc.
📍 Tourist office, 12 cours du 30 juillet 📞 (05) 56 00 66 00
🌐 www.estivales-musique-medoc.com

September

Journées du Patrimoine On the third weekend of the month
many monuments and historic homes open to the public.
📞 (05) 56 00 66 00 🌐 www.bordeaux-tourisme.com

November

Novart A cultural festival with various artists, musicians
and street performers staging events throughout

WHEN TO GO ➜

the city, many of which are free. ☏ (05) 56 10 20 46
🌐 www.bordeaux.fr

December
Christmas Fair Wooden huts and stalls set up around allées
de Tourny selling Christmas decorations, presents and trees.
☏ (05) 56 00 66 00 🌐 www.bordeaux-tourisme.com

PUBLIC HOLIDAYS
Jour de l'An (New Year's Day) 1 January
Lundi de Pâques (Easter Monday) 24 March 2008;
13 April 2009
Fête du Travail (Labour Day) 1 May
Victoire 1945 (World War II Armistice) 8 May
Ascension 22 May 2008; 11 June 2009
Lundi de Pentecôte (Whit Monday) 12 June 2008;
1 June 2009
Bastille Day/Fête Nationale (French Revolution) 14 July
Assomption (Assumption) 15 August
Toussaint (All Saints' Day) 1 November
Armistice 1918 (World War I Armistice) 11 November
Noël (Christmas Day) 25 December

On these days government departments, banks, shops and even
some restaurants are closed.

Wine

Bordeaux is one of the world capitals of wine. The extent of the industry is huge: there are approximately 12,000 winemakers, 8,000 châteaux and 400 wine merchants – not to mention the number of barrel makers, bottle makers, bureaucrats and bar staff – in the Bordeaux area; indeed four out of every ten adults here work in the wine industry in some capacity.

The history of wine in this part of France stretches back over 2,000 years, to when the Romans were planting an ancestor of today's Cabernet Sauvignon grape. Today, there are red, white and rosé (sometimes called *clairet*) wines available, plus a local sparkling wine known as *crémant*. Bordeaux (the wine, not the place) has an unfortunate reputation for being confusing: there are 57 appellations (or regions), and each produces different styles that are bottled and given labels that show the classification, the village, the winemaker... but not the grape. This is because Bordeaux is a blended wine.

The main grape varieties used for blending are actually very well known – Cabernet Sauvignon and Merlot for the reds, Sauvignon Blanc and Semillon for the whites. (In fact 33 per cent of the world's Merlot is grown here, and almost 15 per cent of its Sauvignon Blanc.) The wines from the Left Bank (the Médoc) tend to be richer, longer-lasting and heavier, while those from the Right Bank (Saint Émilion, Pomerol) are more feminine, rounded and can be drunk younger.

Fairs that sell local wines are held locally throughout the year, but before heading out to the vineyards, one of the best ways to get to grips with the subject is to visit the École du Vin (see page 82) for a short introduction, or even the wine bar at the **CIVB** (Bar à Vin, Conseil Interprofessionnel du vin de Bordeaux ⓐ 3 cours du 30 juillet ① (05) 56 00 43 47 ① 10.00–21.00), where they serve glasses of most different regions, and provide maps, books and magazines on the vineyards to peruse while you're having a drink.

◆ *Bordeaux's vineyards are the most important in France*

History

Like most river cities, Bordeaux's story is long and varied. Its proximity to the Atlantic Ocean, coupled with the security offered by its deep, inland harbour, has made it an attractive proposition to settlers for millennia. There are remains of Neanderthal man at the Pair-non-Pair grotto among the vineyards of Premières Côtes de Blaye, and the district of Saint Pierre – today the perfect spot for antiques hunting on a Sunday morning – is located on the exact site of the Roman port of Burdigala.

But it was the commercial links with Britain and northern Europe, forged in earnest after the 12th century when Eleanor of Aquitaine married King Henry II, that saw the city (and its wines) really prosper. After the French victory over the English at Castillon in 1453, the city was united again with France (it had spent a while under English rule), and the focus of trade switched from England to France and northern Europe.

The safe harbour made Bordeaux ideal for trading. In the 18th century it was one of France's wealthiest commercial centres, with the quays of the Chartrons district busy with wine traders from Ireland, Scotland and Holland vying for space in large warehouses storing wood, sugar, coffee and spices from France's colonies. The sweeping line of stone façades, elaborately carved arches and sloping slate roofs along the river front remains almost unchanged, attesting to the wealth of the period. Many of the buildings were designed by Paris's architect, Baron Georges Haussmann.

RESISTANCE BORDEAUX

Although the city was occupied during World War II (and was the scene of the armistice with the Germans in 1940), it also fostered significant pockets of Resistance. The fascinating Centre Jean Moulin (page 64) museum examines the Resistance movement without shirking from confronting the extent of collaboration (on display there's some rather terrifying Nazi memorabilia aimed at convincing the French to stand shoulder to shoulder with the invading army). The museum is named after Jean Moulin, whose sympathies with the Resistance movement forced him into exile in England, from where he coordinated operations and organised a secret army. Parachuted into Provence, he worked for the Resistance until he was finally arrested at Caluire on 21 June 1943. Having been tortured, he died during his transfer from France to Germany.

Bordeaux in the 1970s and 1980s was heavily industrial – the now-gleaming waterfront was down-at-heel, and the Right Bank languished as an industrial desert. In recent years, the city has been the focus of much regeneration, especially since Mayor Alain Juppé came to office in the late 1990s (see Culture, page 22). Twenty-first century Bordeaux is a city that's ready to use the best traditions of its past to equip it for the challenges of the future.

Lifestyle

Some of the clichés associated with Bordeaux – that it is a more reserved city than southern centres such as Marseilles, Nice or Cannes, and that its residents tend to be fairly closed off to newcomers – remain apposite. Perhaps it's something to do with the historical links with the British and northern Europeans, but the Bordelais – to give them their correct name – do tend to dress very smartly, stick to fairly strict social rules, and project an image of being a little closed (at first) to visitors. But increasingly they are embracing their southern French side and – especially if you try speaking a little French – they are very friendly and genuinely happy to welcome you. Some of them are getting used to the new, more glamorous Bordeaux just as much as you are.

The best way to soak up the revitalised lifestyle of Bordeaux is along the quays on a summer day, when the whole city seems to have moved outside, rollerblading or strolling along the river, enjoying the many bars, restaurants and markets there.

The cost of living is fairly reasonable, and cheaper than Paris or London, but it's still a big city, so you do pay a premium. Smoking is widespread, though it's now officially banned in public places such as bars, cafés and restaurants.

Despite its many churches, Bordeaux is not a particularly religious city. That said, opening hours of shops, as in all of France, are still governed by religious laws – there's strictly no opening on Sundays, except for critical shops such as pharmacies (and, this being France, bakeries). France's President, Mr Sarkozy, says he is trying to relax these laws, but for now they still hold true, so be aware of them before heading out on a Sunday with your credit card.

A pleasant shopping street in Bordeaux, with patisserie

Culture

There are many sides to Bordeaux's cultural life: the more traditional aspect has over 20 museums and such institutions as the Grand Théâtre (see page 74) and the medieval courtyard that is the city's most picturesque summer gallery, **Cour Mably** (ⓐ 3 rue Mably ⓣ (05) 56 00 66 00); there is plenty of popular culture, too, from live music in the CAPC Musée d'Art Contemporain (Museum of Contemporary Art, see page 82), to festivals such as the Fête du Vin (see Annual events, page 12). Many events are based around wine – look out for 'Portes Ouvertes' (open door) weekends (see ⓦ www.bordeaux-tourisme.com for details), when wine co-operatives stage cultural entertainments and tastings.

Smaller spaces include the FRAC Gallery (see page 83), the Base Sous-Marine (see page 80), the Cortex Athletico Gallery (see page 64) and the Jardin Botanique (see page 94) in the Bastide.

There are various summer festivals in many of the smaller towns and villages around Bordeaux, such as Jazz in Cussac-Fort-Médoc, staged in the ruins of a fort. The festival is held on the third weekend of July and consists of two days of musical eclecticism (ⓐ Fort Vauban, 33460 Cussac-Fort-Médoc ⓣ (05) 56 58 91 30).

Don't think for a minute that the city's cultural visage is that of the fey aesthete. The relish with which the locals hurl themselves into the annual re-enactment of their humiliation of the English at the battle of Castillon (see page 122), and their prolongation of the celebrations over several weekends, amounts to a good-natured gloat-fest that typifies the Bordelais' inclusive, expansive attitude to celebrating their culture.

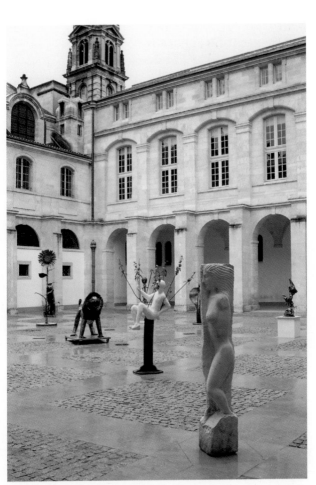

An exhibition of diverse sculpture at Cour Mably

REGENERATION BORDEAUX

The 21st century has so far seen Bordeaux undergo a major renovation, an ongoing project started largely by the Mayor, Alain Juppé, and co-financed by the European Regional Development Fund. Its aim is to regenerate the riverside area using an integrated set of measures involving urban renewal, economic investment and social and cultural development. This has so far resulted in the building of the new tramway, new underground parking, the regeneration of the Right Bank, the planting of parks along the river, large swathes of pedestrianised footways, the sandblasting of all the buildings along the waterfront and the reclamation of the Bassins à Flot and the Marina. The work isn't finished yet – the final parts of the tramway are expected to be laid in 2009 or 2010. Plans for the Marina remain on the drawing board, and there may even be a bridge crossing the Garonne at the Bacalan end of the city; but the city has already changed beyond all recognition.

The wide pavements and spruced up buildings along the riverside

Shopping

Shopping opportunities in Bordeaux have multiplied recently. For clothes, the trendy shops are centred around the 'Golden Triangle' of place des Grands Hommes, allées de Tourny and cours George Clémenceau. Recently smartened-up cours du Chapeau Rouge and cours de l'Intendance are chic, pedestrianised streets, with **Hermès** (ⓐ 2 pl. Gambetta ① (05) 56 52 41 25) and **Le Tanneur** (ⓐ 9 cours de l'Intendance ① (05) 56 81 91 98 ⓦ www.letanneur.com), among many others. More high street shops and Galeries Lafayette (see page 69) are on rue Sainte Catherine, Europe's longest pedestrianised shopping street. For some interesting interiors shops, one-off boutiques and upmarket antique outlets, head over to Chartrons, the old merchant's district.

● *Shopping on rue Sainte Catherine*

Don't leave without exploring rue Faubourg des Arts, where small artisan workshops abound. Past place de la Bourse is Saint Pierre, where you'll find more antiques shops (often offering really good value). The pedestrianised Old Town is full of clothes, interiors, books and gift-shops. Many are centred around place du Parlement, place Camille Jullian and the pretty rue Pas St Georges.

USEFUL SHOPPING PHRASES

What time do the shops (this shop) open/close?
Á quelle heure ouvrent/ferment les magasins (ce magasin)?
Ah kel urr oovra/fairm leh magazahn (suh magazahn)?

Can I try this on?
Puis-je essayer ceci?
Pwee zher ehssayeh suhsee?

My size is...
Ma taille est...
Ma tie eh...

Do you take credit cards?
Prenez-vous les cartes de crédit?
Pruhnay voo leh kart der krehdee?

How much is this?
Ça fait combien?
Sa fay kombyen?

I'll take this one, thank you
Je prends celui-ci/celle-ci merci
Zher prohn selwee-see/sell-see mehrsee

Bigger shopping centres are found in Meriadeck, just north of place Gambetta and on the ring road around the city, notably at Bordeaux Lac, where you'll find everything in the **Auchan complex** (ⓐ Auchan, Centre Commercial Le Lac 33080 ⓣ (05) 56 43 44 00 ⓦ www.auchan.fr) from mobile phone shops to large jewellers.

Markets in Bordeaux are mainly food orientated, but there are several antique fairs held throughout the year, where you'll always have a chance of picking up a nifty bargain.

Eating & drinking

Bordeaux is a gourmet's heaven. The food is typically southwestern – duck, *foie gras* and truffles being the specialities – but there are also lighter options influenced by the nearness of the Atlantic Ocean. The coastal town of Arcachon, 50 km (31 miles) to the west of Bordeaux, farms 60 per cent of France's oysters, and stalls selling them line the streets of the Bordeaux regions of Entre deux Mers and Graves (particularly during the winter months, when oysters are at their best). A great gourmet half-day out is a trip to the oyster beds to watch farmers gathering them early in the morning. (An hour later, you can sample them.)

Back to those regional specialities: duck products are influential, especially *foie gras* (duck liver paté), *magret de canard* (duck breast) and *confit de canard* (duck rillettes). Other local meats include Bazas beef, Pauillac lamb and *grenier médocain*, a kind of spiced pork belly. The most famous local dish is an *entrecôte bordelaise* (steak), with plenty of shallots and red wine sauce.

PRICE CATEGORIES

The following guide indicates the average price per head for a two- to three-course dinner, excluding drinks. Lunch will usually be cheaper, and most restaurants offer a very good value *prix fixe* (fixed price) option between 12.00 and 14.00.
£ up to €25   ££ €26–45   £££ over €45

USEFUL DINING PHRASES

I would like a table for ... people
Je voudrais une table pour ... personnes
Zher voodray oon tabl poor ... pehrson

Waiter/waitress
Monsieur/mademoiselle
M'syer/madmwahzel

Could I have this rare/medium/well cooked
Je le voudrais saignant/à point/bien cuit
Zher ler voodray saynyohn/ah pwan/bi-yen kwee

Can I see the wine list?
La carte des vins s'il vous plaît?
Lah kart day vahn, seel voo pleh?

I am vegetarian
Je suis végétarien/végétarienne
Zher swee vehjaytaryan/vehjaytaryanne

Where are the toilets please?
Où sont les toilettes s'il vous plaît?
Oo son leh twahlet, seel voo pleh?

May I have the bill, please?
L'addition s'il vous plaît
L'adission, seel voo pleh

Fish of all kinds are plentiful. Perhaps the most famous is Lamprey, a fanged eel that's cooked in vast quantities of red wine. The *alose*, or shad, is another native fish, best served simply, grilled in butter over *sarments* (vine cuttings).

Central Bordeaux has a number of wonderful markets. Among the best are the Sunday morning organic market on the quai des Chartrons and the Capucins market (see page 69).

Most of the bars and restaurants are centred around the pedestrianised Old Town and Chartrons, which offers plenty of

⬤ Canelés – *the small caramelised cake from Bordeaux*

CANELÉS AND MACARONS

The sweet specialities of Bordeaux have a long history. Strictly speaking, *canelés* belong to Bordeaux and *macarons* to Saint Émilion, but you'll find both of them accompanying your coffee. *Canelés* are small domed cakes made from batter, caramelised on the outside and soft and creamy on the inside (legend has it that the recipe arose from all the left-over yolks from wine production, as the whites of the eggs were used to filter the wine naturally). Macaroons (or *macarons*) have evolved from a centuries-old recipe, tiny and light made from egg whites, sugar and almonds.

Chinese, Japanese, Indian and Thai establishments to break up the French food. Increasingly the city has realised that wine bars are the way forward. If you want to experiment, the Lillet aperitif (a blend of wine and fruit liqueurs, recommended occasionally by James Bond, incidentally) also comes from Bordeaux.

Bordeaux conforms to the national opening hours – you need to eat lunch between 12.00 and 14.00, at which hour restaurants largely close until around 19.00, with last orders around 22.00.

At almost all restaurants you will be given a *pichet d'eau* when you sit down, a jug of tap water that is perfectly safe to drink.

As is usual in France, a 15 per cent service charge is included in the bill in restaurants, although often not in cafés. It is often customary to add another two to three per cent on top if the service has been good.

Entertainment & nightlife

The good news is that Bordeaux's nocturnal entertainments scene is exploding; the bad news is that the pitiless, survival-of-the-grooviest law of nature means that many of the smaller clubs open up and close down on a regular basis – so it's always worth phoning ahead to check before going.

The recent proliferation of wine bars has been a most welcome phenomenon, and not just because it's put the wine-

luvvies' noses out of joint; try CIVB Wine Bar (see page 15),
Le Bistro du Vingt (see page 72), **Le Petit Bois** (ⓐ rue du Chai
des Farines ⓣ (05) 56 79 06 46) and Le Wine Bar (see page 73).
The main English pubs are found in Chartrons, such as The
Cambridge Arms (see page 89) or near cours Victor Hugo,
where the **Frog and Rosbif** (ⓐ 23 rue Ausone ⓣ (05) 56 48 55 85)
has big video screens to show sporting events. Irish pubs aren't
exactly thin on the ground either – the most lively being Molly

● *Entertainment spots abound near the place de la Bourse*

Malone's (see page 89) and the surreally named **O'Rowlands** (ⓐ 50 rue de Pessac ⓣ (05) 56 99 18 75). For the student bars whose patrons are doing their best to replace the city's wine culture with one built around beer, head to place de la Victoire and the surrounding roads. Bordeaux's best known gay bar is **Bar de l'Hotel de Ville** (ⓐ BHV, 4 rue de l'Hôtel de Ville ⓣ (05) 56 44 05 08).

The more chic bars are found around the Grand Théâtre, the quays around place de la Bourse and Chartrons, and the Triangle d'Or – often a good place to start out an evening. At the far end of quai Bacalan, the Bassins à Flot have a few good nightclubs and a very chic restaurant, La Dame de Shanghai (see page 88), which has a bar and DJ downstairs at weekends. Around Hangar 14 on the quays, lots of new bars and restaurants have opened up recently. Its nightlife scene will be helped enormously now the new tram line has opened up along this top section of the quays. This is definitely an area to watch.

For the later part of your evening, the quai de Paludate is your best bet as most of the clubs, bars and live music venues are around here, from the cavernous **La Distillerie** (ⓐ 96 quai de Paludate ⓣ (05) 56 49 59 49) at the far end of the strip to the ever-popular **Shadow Lounge** (ⓐ 5 rue Cabanac). For a more unusual evening, there's always **Mystic** (ⓐ 5 quai de Paludate ⓣ (05) 56 31 63 24), a dinner/cabaret/club night set in an imposing baroque building.

For live music and great atmosphere, try **Comptoir du Jazz** (ⓐ 59 quai de Paludate ⓣ (05) 56 49 29 12). Other key live music venues include **Rock School Barbey** (ⓐ 18 cours Barbey ⓣ (05) 56 33 66 02 ⓦ www.rockschool-barbey.com), which, if it could be built out of denim, would be.

🔺 *Bordeaux's Grand Théâtre*

There's a casino at Bordeaux Lac (📍 rue Cardinal Richaud 📞 (05) 56 69 49 00), but don't expect Las Vegas. There are plenty of cinemas. For films in *version originale* (look for VO after the title of the film), head for **Utopia** (📍 5 pl. Camille Jullian 📞 (05) 56 52 00 03 🌐 www.cinemas-utopia.org/bordeaux) or **UGC Georges Bonnac** (📍 13–15 rue Georges Bonnac 📞 08 92 89 28 92).

Local listings publications include *Spirit* and *Club et Concerts*, both of which are free monthly publications, available widely in bars and cafés, and often at the tourist office.

Sport & relaxation

The many parks and newly opened quays along the Garonne offer plenty of fresh air potential, and the city's location close to the ocean means there are also plenty of watersports.

SPECTATOR SPORTS

Equestrianism Several large jumping events are held around Bordeaux, especially in Arcachon and Bordeaux Lac.
Jumping International (ⓦ www.bordeaux-expo.com/jumping) is the largest, held at Bordeaux Lac in the first week of February. The **Hippodrome de Bordeaux** (ⓐ av. d'Eysines, Le Bouscat ⓣ (05) 56 28 06 74 ⓦ http://hippodrome.ifrance.com), a reopened track in the smart suburb of Le Bouscat, is a great venue for watching horse racing.

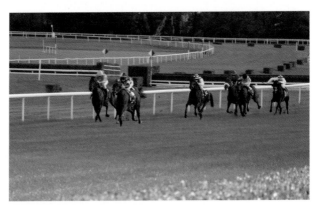

● *Enjoy horse racing at the Hippodrome*

Football Bordeaux's football club is the **FC Girondins**. Their supporters are both vocal and loyal, making any match attendance enormous fun. ⓐ Stade Chaban-Delmas ⓣ Reservations 08 92 68 34 33 ⓦ www.girondins.com

Rugby Rugby is a religion in the southwest of France. The local outfit, **USB-CABBG**, was formed in 2006 and play home matches at the Stade André Moga in Bègles (ⓐ 25 rue Delphin Loche, 33130 ⓣ (05) 56 85 94 01 ⓦ www.cabbg.fr).

PARTICIPATION

Association AIR Rollerblading around the city and skating along the quai des Chartrons are both organised by this excellent group. ⓐ RDV pl. Pey-Berland ⓣ (05) 56 81 21 44 ⓦ www.assoair.com
Centre de Voile This is the best sailing and windsurfing centre in Bordeaux Lac. ⓐ Boulevard du Parc des Expositions, 33520 Bruges ⓣ (05) 57 10 60 35 ⓦ www.voilebordeaux-lac.fr.st

RELAXATION

Piscine Judaïque A recently renovated, large public swimming pool with a gorgeous, art deco interior. ⓐ 166 rue Judaïque ⓣ (05) 56 51 48 31 ⓛ 12.00–14.00, 16.30–19.00 Tues, Fri, 10.00–18.00 Wed, 12.00–14.00, 16.30–21.00 Thur, 12.00–18.00 Sat, 09.00–13.00, 15.00–18.00 Sun, closed Mon
Sources de Caudalie A wine spa – yes, a wine spa – set among the vines of Château Smith Haut Lafitte. Try a Cabernet scrub, a Sauvignon massage, or a jacuzzi in a wine barrel (but mind the splinters). ⓐ Chemin de Smith Haut Lafitte, 33650 Bordeaux-Martillac ⓣ (05) 57 83 83 83 ⓦ www.sources-caudalie.com

Accommodation

Accommodation in Bordeaux hasn't yet caught up with the other improvements in the city – there's a distinct lack of rooms at busy times of year such as the Fête du Vin (see Annual events, page 12). There are plenty of 2- and 3-star hotels, but choices higher up the chain are more limited. There are some interesting *chambre d'hôtes* (bed and breakfasts), and a number of glamorous châteaux to stay in on the outskirts of the city.

Breakfast is often extra, and can be expensive, so you might want to skip it and head to one of the many coffeeshops around the city.

Auberge de la Jeunesse Barbey £ Cheap and cheerful, with kitchen and internet access. Groups need to book one month in advance. **ⓐ** 20 cours Barbey **ⓣ** (05) 56 33 00 70 **ⓦ** www.auberge-jeunesse-bordeaux.com **ⓝ** Tram: Victoire

Hôtel Studio £ Cable TV and showers in every room make this 1-star hotel a good bet. **ⓐ** 26 rue Huguerie **ⓣ** (05) 56 48 00 14 **ⓦ** www.hotel-bordeaux.com/uk/studio.html

PRICE CATEGORIES

The price given is the average for one double room, for one night. Some rates vary during the busy summer months, but Bordeaux doesn't alter its rates too much in high season.

£ up to €50   ££ €50–100   £££ over €100

Hôtel Notre Dame £–££ Simple, well-located hotel, just by the main square in Chartrons. Small bar downstairs. ⓐ 36 rue Notre Dame ⓣ (05) 56 52 88 24 ⓦ www.hotelnotredame.free.fr

Hôtel du Parc £–££ Eight bedrooms, and very simple, but well priced and two minutes from the Jardin Public. ⓐ 10 rue de la Verrerie ⓣ (05) 56 52 78 20

Hôtel Restaurant Le Gambetta £–££ Right by the pretty Porte Dijeaux, this is great for exploring the pedestrianised Old Town. ⓐ 66 rue de la Porte Dijeaux ⓣ (05) 56 51 21 83 ⓦ www.hotel-resto-gambetta.com

Adare House ££ Friendly guesthouse overlooking the Jardin Public. The rooms are individually decorated, and the downstairs one is large, with a small kitchen attached. Wi-Fi in all rooms. ⓐ 91 rue de la Course ⓣ (05) 56 52 48 45 ⓦ www.bordeaux-bnb.com

Une Chambre en Ville ££ Chic, beautifully decorated B&B in the Old Town serving great breakfasts. Only five rooms, so book ahead. ⓐ 35 rue Bouffard ⓣ (05) 56 81 34 53 ⓦ www.bandb-bx.com

Hôtel Burdigala ££ Popular and pristine, and near to Meriadeck shopping centre. ⓐ 115 rue Georges-Bonnac ⓣ (05) 56 90 16 16 ⓦ www.burdigala.com

Hôtel de Normandie ££ Simple, clean and very smart. Located right next to the École du Vin wine school. ⓐ 7 cours du 30 juillet ⓣ (05) 56 52 16 80 ⓦ www.hotel-de-normandie-bordeaux.com

Hôtel des Quatre Soeurs ££ Well located right by the Grand Théâtre, unexceptional (although there are a few large, art deco rooms) but very popular. ⓐ 6 cours du 30 juillet ⓣ (05) 57 81 19 20 ⓦ http://4soeurs.free.fr

La Maison du Lierre ££ Well decorated in a slightly New England style. ⓐ 57 rue Huguerie ⓣ (05) 56 51 66 58 ⓦ www.hotel-maisondulierre-bordeaux.com

Château Grattequina £££ You get to live out the château fantasy in this 19th-century building overlooking the Garonne River in Bacalan. ⓐ av. de Labarde, 33290 Blanquefort ⓣ (05) 56 35 76 76 ⓦ www.grattequina.com

Golf du Médoc Hôtel & Spa £££ Newly opened golf hotel, where you can walk out onto the fairway. Twenty minutes' drive from central Bordeaux. ⓐ chemin de Courmateau, 33290 Le Pian Médoc-Louens ⓣ (05) 56 70 31 31 ⓦ www.hotelgolfduMédoc.com

Hauterive Saint-James £££ Designed by Jean Nouvel, this swish hotel offers Michelin-starred food. ⓐ 3 pl. Camille Hostein, 33270 Bouliac ⓣ (05) 57 97 06 00 ⓦ www.saintjames-bouliac.com

Maison Bord'eaux £££ A city-centre boutique hotel that's a great base for vineyard visitors. ⓐ 113 rue du Docteur Albert Barraud ⓣ (05) 56 44 00 45 ⓦ www.lamaisonbordeaux.com

Petit Hôtel Labottière £££ Slightly shabby living museum on the Right Bank. Just two rooms, both with bathroom. Wonderful inner courtyard for breakfast. ⓐ 14 rue Francis Martin ⓣ (05) 56 48 44 10

The Regent Bordeaux £££ Luxurious finishes on every room, a roof spa, three restaurants and a ballroom make this *the* place to stay; located in the Golden Triangle. ⓐ 2 pl. de la Comédie ⓣ (05) 57 30 44 44 ⓦ www.regenthotels.com

Seekoo Hôtel £££ Niftily designed and sparkling white, this new hotel is the smart choice for a city-centre billet. ⓐ 54 quai Bacalan ⓦ www.seekoo-hotel.com ⓝ Tram: Les Hangars

Sources de Caudalie £££ Sumptious, faux-rustic styling and Chardonnay facials. Two fab restaurants and great views. ⓐ Chemin de Smith Haut Lafitte, 33650 Bordeaux-Martillac ⓣ (05) 57 83 83 83 ⓦ www.sources-caudalie.com

◗ *La Grange au Bateau rooms at Sources de Caudalie*

THE BEST OF BORDEAUX

Whether you're a wine lover, a history buff or a surfer, Bordeaux and its regions offer plenty of tempting options.

TOP 10 ATTRACTIONS

- **Grand Théâtre** Impressive on the outside, gorgeous on the inside; make sure you get cultural in style while you're here (see page 74)

- **The vineyards of Saint Émilion** You can't come to Bordeaux without at least eyeballing a few vines (see page 118)

- **Cathédrale Saint-André & Tour Pey-Berland** Ogle at the 14th-century, double-whammy Gothic wonder of the cathedral and the adjacent bell tower (see page 58)

- **Cuisine** Make the most of the many restaurants around the pedestrianised place du Parlement or the wide stretches of the quai des Chartrons (see Eating & drinking, page 26)

🔽 *The rose window of Cathédrale Saint-André*

- **CAPC Musée d'Art Contemporain (Museum of Contemporary Art)** An art museum that almost vibrates with the energy of its exhibits (see page 82)

- **Quayside architecture** Stroll past the 18th-century buildings that span out on either side from place des Quinconces (see page 80)

- **Jardin Public** The city's most beautiful public park, with botanical gardens, a newly opened café, boat trips around the lake and a museum of natural history (see page 78)

- **Base Sous-Marine** What would you do with a disused U-boat pen? The Bordelais converted theirs into an art space (see page 80)

- **The beaches of Arcachon & the Atlantic Coast** Don't miss chic Cap Ferret and Europe's highest sand dune at the Dune de Pyla (see page 110)

- **The Miroir d'Eau** A reflective water feature opposite the Bourse has turned into a giant paddling pool (see page 62)

Suggested itineraries

HALF-DAY: BORDEAUX IN A HURRY

In summer, take the tram along the quays to place de la Bourse and enjoy the Miroir d'Eau water feature (see page 62). Take a stroll along the quai des Chartrons , where you can eat at one of the many pavement cafés. In winter, substitute the Miroir d'Eau for a trip to the CAPC Museum of Contemporary Art (see page 82).

1 DAY: TIME TO SEE A LITTLE MORE

Once you've done the above, make Cathédrale Saint-André and Tour Pey-Berland (see page 58) your priority – so close that they share an address, the former offers stunning stained glass, the latter fab views. Now you're in the Old Town, spend the afternoon taking in the Centre Jean Moulin (see page 64) to learn about the astonishing exploits of the region's Resistance. Have a rest-those-legs evening and indulge yourself by dining at one of the city's best restaurants, followed by an opera at the Grand Théâtre (see page 74).

2–3 DAYS: TIME TO SEE MUCH MORE

Explore the quays, going right up to the Cap Sciences and the Bassins à Flot. Then visit a *négociant* (wine merchant) that's open to the public and find out a bit more about the infinite subject of wine. Alternatively, get stuck into some shopping with an afternoon in the chic boutiques around the place des Grands Hommes and cours du Chapeau Rouge. In the evening, eat at a restaurant on the allées de Tourny.

LONGER: ENJOYING BORDEAUX TO THE FULL

If you have an extra day, make sure you explore the surrounding countryside and coast. Hire a car or take a train out to Saint Émilion for some vineyard exploration or to Arcachon and the Dune de Pyla for a walk on the beach. Or take a boat taxi down the Garonne.

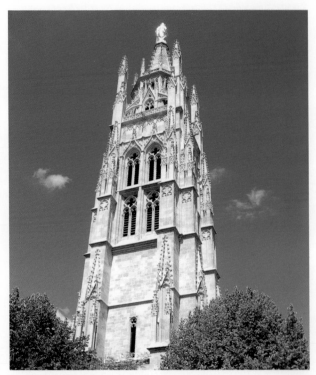

⬤ *Pey-Berland: the first stop on any Bordeaux itinerary*

Something for nothing

Bordeaux has 347 UNESCO World Heritage monuments to explore, almost all of them free, over 20 parks and gardens, and the wide sweep of the Garonne River with animated quays along either side (a 6-km/4-mile walk has recently been opened that explores the entire length). This means there is more than enough open space for wandering around that won't cost you a thing. Among the many parks, the Jardin Public (see page 78) and the Parc Bordelais (see page 78) are especially good for children, with Punch and Judy shows and pony rides in summer. For people-watching, try the Skate Park (see page 134), the Jardin des Lumières (see page 62) and the Miroir d'Eau (see page 62) along the river front. The Jardin Botanique (see page 94) over on the Right Bank is another lovely park for wandering around, with its zen-like water features.

On the first Sunday of every month, art galleries are free. The city centre is also closed to cars on the same day, and there are often small street markets and a variety of entertainments laid on. Many museums are in fact free throughout the month, including the Musée d'Aquitaine (see page 66) and the Musée des Beaux Arts (see page 66). But do note that temporary exhibitions almost always have a charge.

Among the many examples of fine 18th-century architecture, seek out Jacques Gabriel's Allées de Tourny (see page 74), Victor Louis' Grand Théâtre (see page 74) and Richard Rogers' **Court of First Instance** (② pl. République ① (05) 56 01 34 20). In Quartier Saint Eloi, at the end of cours de l'Intendance, you can see Montaigne's old house at 23–25 rue de la Rousselle.

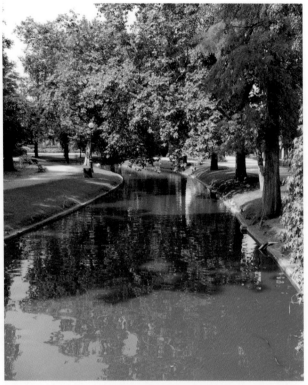

⬧ *Relax and meander through one of Bordeaux's many parks*

The markets are all free entry, and certainly make for a fascinating couple of people-watching, bargain-spotting hours; you don't have to buy anything. The best outdoor ones are in Saint Pierre and Saint Michel on weekend mornings.

When it rains

Bordeaux's location just inland from the Atlantic Ocean means it is no stranger to rainy days. One of the best things to do is to get out into the vineyards and visit a few properties – among the best for non wine specialists is La Winery (see page 99) about 25 minutes north of Bordeaux in the Médoc.

The many beautiful churches that are dotted throughout the city centre will provide some spectacular environments in which to shelter and, indeed, totally forget about such trifles as the weather. **Saint Michel** (❷ pl. Duborg), and **Saint-Seurin** (❸ 13 rue Ernest Renan) are UNESCO World Heritage Sites, and Église St Louis des Chartrons (see page 83) has free concert recitals on Sunday afternoons. The city's main cathedral, Cathédrale Saint-André (see page 58), has stunning stained-glass windows.

Alternatively, get a culture fix at a museum – you can look at the archaeological heritage of the area at the Musée d'Aquitaine (see page 66), indulge in some art gazing at the Musée des Beaux Arts (see page 66), or go avant-garde at the CAPC Museum of Contemporary Art (see page 82).

No rainy day is complete without some shopping – what a great excuse. Pas St Georges's books and clothes shops constitute a legitimate alternative to the frizzies, as does the array of stores at Meriadeck indoor shopping centre (see page 68), which also has some lovely snack-points. Once you're all shopped out, head to Cinéma Utopia (see page 33) to catch an English-language film.

You could also embrace the rain by going to the Miroir d'Eau (see page 62) to really splash in puddles, or take a swim at the Piscine Judaïque (see page 35).

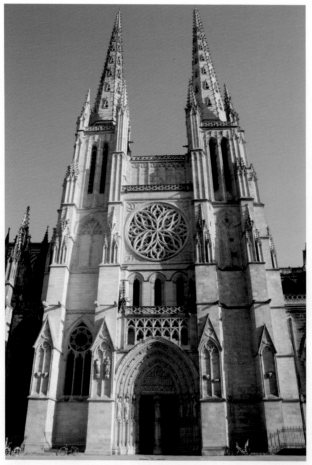

● Bordeaux's cathedral provides a captivating (and dry) glimpse into the past

On arrival

TIME DIFFERENCE
Bordeaux is on European standard time (GMT plus one hour).
Daylight saving is exactly the same as in the rest of Europe –
clocks go forward an hour in spring, and back an hour in autumn.

ARRIVING
By air
The international airport in Bordeaux is called **Bordeaux-Mérignac**
(❶ (05) 56 34 50 50 ⓦ www.bordeaux-airport.com), and it's situated
around 10 km (6 miles) outside the city. There are flights to and
from a variety of international cities by airlines including British
Airways, Air France, bmibaby, easyJet, Flybe and Ryanair.

From the airport, buses and taxis go to the city centre, and
the taxi rank is on the arrivals level of Hall B. Fares are €25–45.
Call **Taxi Mérignac** (❶ (05) 56 97 11 27).

A bus connects the airport to Gare St-Jean (see below),
leaving every 45 minutes from Terminal B, 07.45–22.45. The
return service departs from 06.45–21.45. Tickets are €6.80,
phone ❶ (05) 56 34 50 50 for details.

By rail
The main TGV train station in Bordeaux is **Gare St-Jean** (ⓐ rue
Charles Domercq ❶ Info & reservations 3635 ⓦ www.voyages-
sncf.com), which is about 4 km (just over 2 miles) outside the
city centre, on the Left Bank of the Garonne River. Trains arrive
from all over France, including at least six a day from Paris. The
tram line that goes to place des Quinconces in central Bordeaux

starts directly outside, and the tourist office is opposite the tram stop at Quinconces.

By road

The bus station is in the city centre, at the **Hatte Routière terminal** (ⓐ allées de Chartres), where most of the buses into and around Bordeaux start and stop. Most buses are run by Trans'Gironde.

Access by car comes from Paris on the A10, and up from Toulouse on the A62, and from Arcachon, Biarritz and Spain on the A63. For traffic information when you travel, phone **Traffic info** ⓣ 08 05 90 33 33

⊙ *The main station in Bordeaux – Gare St-Jean*

The many underground car parks give excellent access to the main shopping areas. Expect to spend €10–15 for a full day's parking.

By water
The nearest international passenger ferry ports are at Caen up in northern France, or Santander down in Spain, from where travel would have to be by road or rail.

FINDING YOUR FEET
Bordeaux is a safe city by pretty much any standard. You might want to be careful around the train station and quai de Paludate or quai Bacalan at night, but other than that, the usual warnings about pickpockets and traffic apply.

There are some great tours offered by the Office de Tourisme. The UNESCO Tour runs by bus at night a few times a week during the summer and visits the key monuments. There are also guided walks, bike tours, horse-drawn carriage tours, architecture tours and gourmet tours. If you're visiting several sights, the 'Bordeaux Pass' gives access to various attractions. Details are available from the tourist office (see page 137).

ORIENTATION
Bordeaux is divided in two by the Garonne River. The easiest way to get your bearings is to work out where the river is – and thus place des Quinconces, the largest square in the city that divides the Old Town from Chartrons and Bacalan.

GETTING AROUND
There are three tram lines – A, B and C – that link the train station

IF YOU GET LOST, TRY...

Sorry to bother you, but...
Excusez-moi de vous déranger, mais...
Ekskezay-mwah der voo dayronjay, may...

Could you tell me the way to...
Comment fait-on pour aller à ...
Kohmohn feyt-ohn poor al-lay ah ...

Do you speak English?
Parlez-vous anglais?
Pahrlay-voo ahnglay?

Could you point to it on my map?
Pouvez-vous me le montrer sur la carte?
Poo vay voo muh ler montray soor lah kart?

with place des Quinconces in the central area, and travel back out to the suburbs of Pessac and Mérignac Centre and the far end of the quays, the Bassins à Flot. Locals often call the trams the metro.

Line A runs from the Mérignac Centre to Lormont Lauriers or Floirac Dravemont. This line goes through the centre of Bordeaux, passing the cathedral at place Pey-Berland and out to the Bastide and the Jardin Botanique.

Line B runs from Pessac Centre to the Bassins à Flot. This line goes along the quai des Chartrons, and on past place de la Victoire.

Line C runs from the Gare St-Jean to place des Quinconces, with the extension to the Grand Parc. The new extension will pass through the Jardin Public and Chartrons.

The trams are modern, clean and very attractive – make sure that you buy a ticket in advance and validate it once you get on board. A single trip costs €1.20, or you can buy passes of five or ten. Once you've validated, you can change trams for up to one hour. There are also a large number of bus routes crossing the city. Both tram and bus are run by **Réseau Connex** (🛈 (05) 57 57 88 88 🌐 www.infotbc.com).

Bordeaux has a number of taxi firms, including:

Allô Bordeaux 🛈 (05) 56 31 61 07 🌐 www.ciao.fr

Aquitaine Cars 🛈 (05) 56 86 80 30 🌐 www.aquitaine-cars.com

Water taxis are an excellent and unusual way of getting around, and these are run by **Clapotine** (🖂 quai des Queyries 🛈 (06) 07 19 75 86 🌐 www.evolutiongaronne.com 🚊 Tram: Stalingrad).

CAR HIRE

The main car hire companies are found at the train station and the airport. There are a few cheaper companies on the roads leading up to the station, but the big guys are all directly outside.

Europcar 🛈 Bordeaux-Mérignac Airport (05) 56 34 05 79; Gare St-Jean 08 25 00 42 46 🌐 www.europcar.fr

Hertz 🛈 Bordeaux-Mérignac Airport (05) 56 34 59 87; Gare St-Jean (05) 57 59 05 95 🌐 www.hertz.fr

Sixt 🛈 Bordeaux-Mérignac Airport (05) 56 34 08 15 🌐 www.sixt.fr

---

▶ *The romanesque Three Graces fountain on Place de la Bourse*

The Old Town, Saint Pierre & Saint Michel

This is the historical heart of Bordeaux, where the pedestrianised Old Town meets cobbled squares and tiny streets filled with churches and market places, next to modern bars and student hang-outs. The majority of the UNESCO World Heritage monuments are crowded into these streets, and much of the recent renovation work has been concentrated here.

SIGHTS & ATTRACTIONS

Cathédrale Saint-André & Tour Pey-Berland

A 13th-century cathedral that's been half renovated, giving a stripe of clean limestone surrounded by darker, dirtier stone. The stunning interior has excellent stained-glass windows. Alongside it is the Tour Pey-Berland, a bell tower that's also open to the public. ⓐ pl. Pey-Berland ⓣ (05) 56 87 17 18 ⓛ 10.00–18.00 June–Sept; 10.00–12.00, 14.00–17.00 Oct–May ⓝ Tram: Hôtel de Ville

Église Saint-Pierre

An imposing, Gothic-looking structure that dates from the 15th century and has additions from the 19th. ⓐ pl. Saint Pierre ⓣ (05) 56 52 24 68 ⓝ Tram: Place de la Bourse

Grosse Cloche

The Saint Eloi gate looks almost Austrian in style, with its clock and bell. Today, it opens out onto the chic shops of rue Saint James. ⓐ rue Saint James ⓝ Tram: Porte de Bourgogne

⏶ *The gothic allure of the Grosse Cloche*

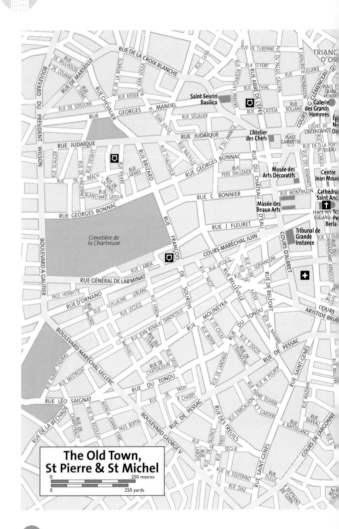

The Old Town,
St Pierre & St Michel

0 _____ 250 metres
0 _____ 250 yards

Place de la Bourse & the Miroir d'Eau

Fresh from renovations and one of the best urban regeneration projects in the city, the Miroir d'Eau is a huge, shallow water feature that reflects the classic 18th-century buildings and smart central fountain of the place de la Bourse. The water alternates between spray, jets and a shallow pool, and on sunny days seems to attract half the children of the city. The flowerbeds of the Jardin des Lumières surround it on either side. ⓐ pl. de la Bourse Ⓝ Tram: Place de la Bourse

Place Camille Jullian

Another lively pedestrianised square in the centre of the Old Town, full of cafés and bars, but also the Utopia cinema (see page 33), the best art-house cinema in Bordeaux. Ⓝ Tram: Place de la Bourse

Place du Parlement

The fountain at the centre of this pedestrianised square is surrounded by children playing all summer. There are restaurants stuffed into almost every corner, interspersed with the odd bookshop or clothes shop, and beautiful 18th-century houses. Ⓝ Tram: Place de la Bourse

Porte Cailhau

This elaborately carved stone gate was built in 1495, and marks the entrance along the quays to the Saint Pierre district. You can even explore inside it. ⓐ pl. du Palais Ⓛ 14.00–19.00 June–Sept, closed Oct–May Ⓝ Tram: Porte de Bourgogne

ÉCHOPPES

As you walk around the residential parts of Saint Pierre, Saint Eloi and the Old Town, it's hard to miss the low-lying stone houses that line the streets, opening straight onto the pavement with no front garden. This is the typical Bordeaux house, and is called an *échoppe*. These are usually one-storey, low, wide stone buildings that were built between the 15th and 18th century as workers' and artisans' housing, but are now considered very chic, and are often beautifully restored. The architecture is very similar for all *échoppes* – usually with a walled town garden at the back, no garden at the front, a large, elaborately carved wooden front door and a symmetrical layout inside, where you have two identical living rooms on either side of a rising central stair looking out onto the road, then the kitchen and living quarters at the back, opening onto the quieter garden. Some of the best examples in Bordeaux are found in Sacré Coeur (off Rue de l'Ecole Normale), Nansouty, Saint Augustin (off Allée des Pins), Camille Godard and Talence.

CULTURE

L'Atelier des Chefs

Here you'll find cultural instruction in the form of Bordeaux-style cooking classes where you get to enjoy the finished product over a glass of wine. There's also a great shop selling cookery books and accessories. 🅐 25 rue Judaïque 🅣 (05) 56 00 72 70 🅦 www.atelierdeschefs.com 🅛 10.00–19.00 🅝 Tram: Gambetta

Centre Jean Moulin

The museum of the Resistance movement was set up to give a balanced view. Thus the deportation of the Jews and other dark episodes from World War II are illustrated alongside the heroics performed by the Free French Forces. 🅐 48 pl. Jean Moulin, rue Vital Carles 🅣 (05) 56 79 66 00 🅦 www.centrejeanmoulin.com 🅛 11.00–18.00 Tues–Fri, 14.00–18.00 Sat & Sun, closed Mon 🅝 Tram: Hôtel de Ville

Cortex Athletico Gallery

A large area given over to two sections, one offering workshop space to visiting artists, the other dedicated to permanent exhibitions. 🅐 1 rue des Étables 🅣 (05) 56 94 31 89 🅦 www.cortexathletico.com 🅛 Thur–Sat 14.00–20.00, closed Sun–Wed 🅝 Tram: Sainte Croix

Millésima

This central wine merchant's warehouse is the place to learn all about the city's all-pervasive wine culture. There's a wine school available, and tours offering an insight into the Bordeaux system of selling through wine merchants. There are also over two million bottles in the cellar and a stylish shop where you can kit yourself out as an oenologist. 🅐 87 quai de Paludate 🅣 (05) 57 80 88 08 🅦 www.millesima.fr 🅛 Appointment preferred 🅝 Tram: Sainte Croix

◆ *Bordeaux is any wine lover's dream destination*

Musée d'Aquitaine

A museum that takes an extensive look at the archaeology and history of the area, but also at the cultural influences that have shaped modern-day Bordeaux. There are recreations of Roman mosaic floors a-plenty. 20 cours Pasteur (05) 56 01 51 00 11.00–18.00 Wed–Sun, closed Mon & Tues Tram: Musée d'Aquitaine

Musée des Arts Décoratifs

A lovely cobbled courtyard marks the entrance to this small, elegant museum, displaying collections of jewellery, glassware and paintings. 39 rue Bouffard (05) 56 10 14 00 14.00–18.00 Wed–Sun, closed Mon & Tues Tram: Sainte Catherine

Musée des Beaux Arts

One of the most impressive buildings of all the city's museums, this 16th-century structure lies in the middle of the gardens of the Hôtel de Ville. Permanent and temporary exhibitions, split over two galleries, include works by Rubens and Titian, alongside those by more modern artists such as Picasso and Dufy. 20 cours d'Albret (05) 56 96 61 50 11.00–18.00 Wed–Mon, closed Tues Tram: Hôtel de Ville

Musée National des Douanes

By place de la Bourse, this former tax office for passing shipping trade is now a museum looking at the history of that area of commerce in the region. 1 pl. de la Bourse (05) 56 48 82 82 10.00–18.00 Wed–Sun, closed Mon & Tues Tram: Place de la Bourse

Tribunal de Grande Instance

Designed by Richard Rogers in 1998, this glass-and-stainless-steel creation proves that Bordeaux's architectural golden age didn't end in the 18th century. ⓐ rue des Frères Bonie Ⓝ Tram: Hôtel de Ville

RETAIL THERAPY

Bordeaux's Old Town is full of small, interesting shops in which to spend a few (dozen) hours. As you would expect, there is a high density of wine shops, most of which offer shipping overseas. Running between place du Parlement and place Camille Jullian, rue du Pas St Georges is a treasure trove of clothes shops, card shops, hairdressers, bookshops, newsagents, cafés and interior design places. The smart street of rue Bouffard is known for its antique stores, and also has some good interior design shops.

Bayonne Chocolate shop Delicious chocolates made from a town around two hours south of Bordeaux, approaching the Spanish border. The signature is a dark, spicy chocolate. ⓐ 6 rue des Remparts ⓣ (05) 56 44 55 72 ⓛ 09.30–13.00, 14.30–18.00 Mon–Sat, closed Sun Ⓝ Tram: Sainte Catherine; bus: 4

Les Caves d'Ausone Wine shop owned by a journalist from top wine mag *Revue des Vins de France* – a good mix of wine, glasses, decanters and gourmet books. ⓐ 2 pl. du Palais ⓣ (05) 56 48 53 08 ⓛ 10.00–12.00, 15.00–18.00 Tues–Sat, closed Sun & Mon Ⓝ Tram: Porte de Bourgogne

Centre Meriadeck Large and central shopping centre,
with a supermarket and also a range of smaller, more
interesting shops. ⓐ rue du Château d'Eau ⓣ (05) 56 93 00 15
ⓛ 09.30–20.00 Mon–Sat, 10.30–16.00 Sun ⓝ Tram: Meriadeck

Cousin & Compagnie A friendly, well-designed wine
shop stocking bottles from Spain, Italy and further afield,
as well as well-chosen boutique wines from around Bordeaux.
Knowledgeable, often English-speaking staff and regular
tasting evenings. ⓐ 2 rue de Pas St Georges ⓣ (05) 56 01 20 23
ⓦ www.cousin.fr ⓛ 16.00–22.00 Mon–Sat, 14.00–20.00 Sun
ⓝ Tram: Place de la Bourse

🔺 Bordeaux's food markets are among the finest in Europe

MARKETS

If you like your fodder fresh, an early-start trip to Capucins market will be just the job. This is the place where the local restaurants buy their food, and, when you've bought yours, grab an early brunch at the delicious oyster bar. ⓐ pl. des Capucins ⏱ 05.00–13.00 Tues–Sun, closed Mon Ⓝ Tram: Sainte Croix

Your inner David Dickinson will thank you for a jaunt to Passage Saint Michel, where you'll find bric-a-brac or antique stalls out on the square in front of the Saint Michel basilica, and around 40 different dealers displaying their wares inside this charming antique centre. ⓐ 14–17 pl. Canteloup ☎ (05) 56 92 14 76 ⏱ 09.30–18.30 Mon–Sat, 08.00–14.00 Sun Ⓝ Tram: Porte de Bourgogne

Galeries Lafayette France's signature department store has two buildings in this part of Bordeaux – one for women and one for men. In the main (women's) building, there's a good café on the third floor. ⓐ 11 rue Sainte Catherine ☎ (05) 56 44 46 59 Ⓦ www.galerieslafayette.fr ⏱ 10.00–19.00 Mon–Sat, closed Sun Ⓝ Tram: Grand Théâtre

Zara In case you haven't brought enough holiday clothes, rest assured there's a Zara! ⓐ 33 rue Porte Dijeaux ☎ (05) 56 00 61 35 ⏱ 10.00–19.00 Mon–Sat, closed Sun Ⓝ Tram: Sainte Catherine

TAKING A BREAK

L'Echappée Belle £ ❶ Coffees, teas, smoothies, salads... run by an English/French husband/wife team. Well located near the Utopia Cinema. ⓐ 41 rue du Pas St Georges ⓣ (05) 56 44 40 79 Ⓝ Tram: Place de la Bourse

Restaurant Karl £ ❷ One of the most relaxed and fun breakfast spots in town. Long wooden benches and large windows make this a café that you could find in Sydney or Barcelona, and there's a great range of patisseries, breads, and larger snacks. Excellent soups and salads at lunchtime. ⓐ pl. du Parlement ⓣ (05) 56 81 01 00 Ⓛ 08.30–19.30 Mon–Sat, closed Sun Ⓝ Tram: Place de la Bourse

Cafés des Arts £–££ ❸ Classic French bistro fare in the student quarter with a lively bar attached. ⓐ 138 cours

● Go to Karl for a great breakfast or lunch

Victor Hugo ☎ (05) 56 91 78 46 ⏱ 12.00–14.00, 19.00–23.00 Ⓝ Tram: Musée d'Aquitaine

Couleurs Sucrées £–££ ❹ There's a wide choice of herbal teas and sweet treats at this welcoming *salon de thé*. ⓐ 12 rue du Parlement Saint Pierre ☎ (05) 56 79 30 90 ⏱ 10.00–21.00 Mon–Sat, 10.00–19.00 Sun Ⓝ Tram: Place de la Bourse

Le Grand Castan £–££ ❺ Perfectly located on the quays, opposite the Miroir d'Eau, this eccentric bar was opened in the 19th century and has a grotto-style back wall (they love this effect in Bordeaux for some reason) and a good range of drinks and cocktails. ⓐ 2 quai de la Douane ☎ (05) 56 44 51 97 ⏱ 10.00–19.00 Mon–Sat, closed Sun Ⓝ Tram: Place de la Bourse

AFTER DARK

RESTAURANTS
Moshi Moshi ££–£££ ❻ Excellent Japanese restaurant housed in an old cellar. The downstairs toilets are worth the trip alone, with their mini Zen gardens and water dripping out of bamboo shoots. ⓐ 8 pl. Fernand Lafargue ☎ (05) 56 79 22 91 ⏱ 20.00–23.00 Tues–Sat, closed Sun & Mon Ⓝ Tram: Porte de Bourgogne

L'Oenotria ££–£££ ❼ A gourmet wine restaurant, with champagne bar upstairs and excellent range of good quality wines by the glass. ⓐ 12 rue d'Ausone ☎ (05) 56 79 30 30 ⏱ 12.00–14.00, 20.00–22.30 Tues–Sat, closed Sun & Mon Ⓝ Tram: Porte de Bourgogne

● *Le Grand Castan is one of the popular café bars on the quays*

La Tupina ££–£££ ❹ One of Bordeaux's best-loved bistros, where mega-chef Jean Pierre Xaradakis presides over his open fire, cooking up chunks of meat that wouldn't be out of place on Tony Soprano's table. ⓐ 12 rue Porte de la Monnaie ① (05) 56 91 56 37 ⓦ www.latupina.com ⓛ 12.00–14.00, 19.00–23.00 ⓝ Tram: Sainte Croix

PUBS, BARS & CLUBS
Le Bistro du Vingt One of a number of new wine bars to open up in the past few years. Very relaxed downstairs bar with a variety of wines available by the glass, many from Spain and Italy. Range of Spanish hams to accompany – and a bistro upstairs. ⓐ 20 rue des Piliers de Tutelle (off Rue St-Remi) ① (05) 56 52 49 79

🕐 12.00–14.00, 19.00–22.30 Tues–Sat, closed Sun & Mon
🚊 Tram: Grand Théâtre

Café Brun Great atmosphere at this Irish-vibed bar, which serves some of the best Guinness in town. 🅰 45 rue Saint-Rémi 📞 (05) 56 52 20 49 🕐 12.00–01.00 Tues–Sat, closed Sun & Mon 🚊 Tram: Place de la Bourse

Le Factory Cavernous club with big-name visiting DJs and a regular, young crowd. Two floors, both entirely given over to house, electro and garage music. 🅰 88 quai de Paludate 📞 (05) 56 49 10 00 🌐 www.le-factory.com 🕐 10.00–04.00 Thur–Sat, closed Sun–Wed 🚊 Tram: Sainte Croix

Le Furax Relatively new and glamorous club, with an up-for-it student crowd. 🅰 68 quai de Paludate 📞 (05) 56 89 47 33 🕐 10.00–02.00 Wed–Sat, closed Sun–Tues 🚊 Tram: Sainte Croix

Saintex Big music venue with regular live concerts. 🅰 54 cours de la Marne 📞 (05) 56 31 21 04 🌐 http://saintex33.free.fr 🕐 21.00–02.00 Wed–Sat, closed Sun–Tues 🚊 Tram: Hôtel de Ville

Le Wine Bar Slightly out of the way new wine bar that has a good range by the glass. It's on one of the winding (driveable) roads on the outskirts of the pedestrianised centre. 🅰 19 rue Bahutiers 📞 (05) 56 48 56 99 🕐 12.00–14.00, 19.00–22.00 Tues–Sat, closed Sun & Mon 🚊 Tram: Porte de Bourgogne

THE CITY

Golden Triangle, Jardin Public, Chartrons & Bacalan

Chic and well-heeled, the Triangle d'Or (Golden Triangle) and the Jardin Public are the places to go for window shopping, admiring both the glamorous objects to buy, and the glamorous Bordelaises enjoying *la belle vie française*. Moving up into Chartrons, things get slightly grungier, as this former merchant and artist quarter has more narrow streets and tiny shops; but it is increasingly trendy and expensive, and now one of the liveliest, most rewarding districts of the city. Bacalan, further up again, is promisingly up and coming but still has a way to go.

SIGHTS & ATTRACTIONS

Allées de Tourny

A pretty square that leads onto the Grand Théâtre. Together they mark the far side of the pedestrianised Old Town, and the crossover into the chic Triangle d'Or district. Some of the city's smartest restaurants are housed around this square, together with the wine school and many wine shops, while the central space has a carousel and hosts the annual summer food fair and winter Christmas fair (see Annual events, page 13). ◍ Tram: Grand Théâtre

Grand Théâtre

Perhaps the city's most famous sight, this beautiful building was designed by Victor Hugo and opened in 1780. Corinthean columns line one side, and an art deco-style bar and café serves drinks and

Ornate decoration in the atrium of the Grand Théâtre

Golden Triangle,
Jardin Public, Chartrons
& Bacalan

bistro-style food. Opera, classical concerts and ballet are performed throughout the year. pl. de la Comédie (05) 56 00 85 90 Guided visits available, phone (05) 56 00 66 00 to arrange Tram: Grand Théâtre

Jardin Public

Ducks on the pond, classical music on the carousel, a large children's play area, a museum of natural history, a library, an excellent café, a botanical garden, formal flowerbeds and loads of grass: now that's what we call a park. pl. du Champ de Mars; entrances on cours de Verdun, rue du Jardin Public rue d'Aviau, pl. Bardineau 07.00–20.00 (spring & autumn); 07.00–21.00 (summer); 07.00–18.00 (winter) Tram: Jardin Public; bus: 31

Palais Gallien

Best preserved of the Roman ruins right in the city centre, dating back to the 2nd century. It was originally an amphitheatre capable of holding 17,000 people. It's well hidden down a side street, but worth seeking out, even though only a few walls remain – basically the entrance to the original amphitheatre. rue du Palais Gallien Bus: 53

Parc Bordelais

The largest park in the city, just on the other side of the boulevards by the Barrière du Médoc. There's a river, an animal park, a little train, lots of swans and ducks and a Punch and Judy theatre. rue du Bocage. Entrances also on rue du Parc 07.00–20.00 (spring & autumn), 07.00–21.00 (summer); 07.00–18.00 (winter) Bus: 57, 58

CHARTRONS

The area of Chartrons has a colourful history, bound up with immigrants of all nationalities, most often from Ireland, Scotland, England and Holland. They arrived in Bordeaux mainly between the 17th and 18th centuries to trade cocoa, spices, teas, coffees, sugar and wine between Europe, America and the French colonies in Africa and the Caribbean. Buildings such as the CAPC Museum of Contemporary Art began life as an *entrepôt*, or sugar warehouse. At the end of the 19th century, the city's mayor, Lodi-Martin Duffour-Dubergier, proclaimed, '*L'âme de Bordeaux, c'est le commerce*' ('The soul of Bordeaux is trade') – and Chartrons was where most of it went on. As wine merchants moved out of the city centre to expand their warehouses and bottling lines in areas where land was less expensive, so Chartrons spent many years with increasingly blackened walls and empty shop fronts, but today commerce, and plenty of residents, have moved back in, and these few square miles contain some of the highest property prices in the region.

Parc Rivière

This is a great place to escape from the city for a few hours. Of particular interest are the ruins of a 19th-century château.
ⓐ rue de Rivière ⏲ 07.00–20.00 (spring & autumn); 07.00–21.00 (summer); 07.00–18.00 (winter)
Ⓝ Bus: 27, 57, 58

Place des Quinconces

Among Europe's biggest pedestrianised squares, this elegant, tree-lined expanse features a striking fountain and statues of Montaigne and Montesquieu, two of Bordeaux's most famous sons. Esplanade de Quinconces Tram: Quinconces

Quai des Chartrons

The first of the quays to be renovated, this has wide pavements filled with cafés and restaurants running alongside the river. Attractions include a skate park, a children's biking area and some good playgrounds. Tram: Chartrons

Saint-Seurin Basilica

Just to the north of Gambetta and the city centre is one of the most striking examples of religious architecture you'll find. Recent renovations show off the elaborate carvings inside and out. An 11th-century crypt holds an early-Christian necropolis, with mausoleums, sarcophagus and frescos. pl. des Martyrs de la Résistance Bus: 83

CULTURE

Base Sous-Marine (Submarine Pen)

Built by the Nazis during World War II to house their U-boats, this impressive concrete structure is strangely haunting. There's an exhibition of the submarines inside, plus an art gallery as part of the complex, and cultural events and music nights are held regularly. blvd Alfred Daney (05) 56 11 11 50 13.00–19.00 Wed-Sun, closed Mon & Tues Tram: Bassins à Flot

◆ *The ornate fountain at Place des Quinconces*

Cap Sciences

At the far end of the quays, the science and natural history museum is housed in a modern building and contains fun and interactive exhibits on everything from space travel to how computers work. @ Hangar 20 quai Bacalan ① (05) 56 01 07 07 Ⓦ www.cap-sciences.net ⏱ 14.00–18.00 Tues–Fri, 14.00–19.00 Sat & Sun, closed Mon Ⓝ Tram: Les Hangars

CAPC Musée d'Art Contemporain (Museum of Contemporary Art)

This stunning space has been open since the 1980s, and contains a mix of permanent works (look out for Keith Haring's *Baby in the Lift*) and changing exhibitions. The excellent café does the best Sunday brunch around. @ 7 rue Ferrère ① (05) 56 00 81 50 ⏱ 11.00–18.00 Tues, Thur–Sun, 11.00–20.00 Wed, closed Mon Ⓝ Tram: CAPC. Admission charge

École du Vin

The official wine school of Bordeaux that runs two- and three-hour classes, special courses focusing on food and wine matching or blending, or longer three- or four- dayers that divide their time between the classroom and the vineyards. @ CIVB, 1 cours du 30 juillet ① (05) 56 00 22 66 Ⓦ www.ecole.vins-bordeaux.fr Ⓝ Tram: Quinconces

Église Notre Dame

Just next to the Grand Hommes shopping centre, you could easily miss this beautiful, baroque-style church as it's hidden in an attractive square sandwiched between chic clothing shops. Concerts and organ recitals are held regularly. @ pl. du Chapelet ⏱ 07.00–20.00 Ⓝ Tram: Grand Théâtre

Église St Louis des Chartrons

Beautiful Catholic church in the heart of Chartrons, dating back to the 14th century, although the current neo-Gothic structure was constructed in 1880. It holds free concerts most Sunday afternoons. Due to the high number of immigrants traditionally living in Chartrons, from English and Irish merchants to Dutch missionaries, it was known in the 18th century as the 'Foreigner's Church'. ⓐ rue Notre Dame ⓛ Service 10.30 Sun
Ⓜ Tram: Place Paul Doumer; bus: 31, 4

The FRAC Gallery

This is a free exhibition space that regularly holds contemporary photography, sculpture and video exhibits, often favouring regional artists. Since 1983, FRAC (regional art collections) have appeared in many cities all over France, created to promote the visual arts as well as decentralising the Paris-based art network. ⓐ Hangar G2, Bassins à Flot no. 1, quai Armand Lalande ⓣ (05) 56 24 71 36 Ⓦ www.fracaquitaine.net
Ⓜ Tram: Bassins à Flot

Le Garage Moderne

Proving that the most uplifting things can be found in the most unlikely of places, this unusual building is a working garage that doubles as an exhibition space. You can take your car in to be repaired, get a hands-on lesson in how to repair it, end up discussing your favourite artist or admiring an exhibition of sculptures that is displayed among the rusting bumpers. ⓐ 1 rue des Étrangers ⓣ (05) 56 50 91 33
Ⓦ www.legaragemoderne.org Ⓜ Tram: Bassins à Flot

RETAIL THERAPY

The shopping experience in this area is a pleasantly sedate one. Small antique shops, furniture restorers and larger antique showrooms abound on rue Notre Dame. Rue Faubourg des Arts, at the top of cours Portal, is a gem: an artists' street, entirely given over to small workshops and artisan boutiques, from sculptures to lighting specialists to seamstresses.

Chez Antoine The best pâtisserie in town, where simple sugar creations turn into little pieces of gourmet heaven. Try their brightly coloured macaroons. ⓐ 19 cours Portal ⓣ (05) 56 81 43 19 ⓛ 08.00–20.00 Mon–Sat, 08.00–13.00 Sun ⓝ Tram: Place Paul Doumer

Galerie des Grands Hommes One of the most chic central shopping centres – housed in a glass rotunda, with streets heading off, all named after the *grands hommes* Montesquieu and Voltaire. Inside is a mix of shops hawking food, toys, interiors and clothes. ⓐ pl. des Grands Hommes ⓛ 10.00–20.00 Mon–Sat, closed Sun ⓝ Tram: Grand Théâtre; bus: 4

Jean d'Alos If you want to buy cheese, explore cheese, admire cheese or sample cheese, this is the place to come. The same shop has a branch in Chartrons, on cours Portal. ⓐ 4 rue Montesquieu (off Cours de l'Intendance) ⓣ (05) 56 44 29 66 ⓝ Tram: Grand Théâtre; bus: 4

Mac Makeup Just one of the many chic shops that line cours Georges Clémenceau, one of the outer points of the

Triangle d'Or. ⓐ 14 cours Georges Clémenceau ⓣ (05) 57 30 00 00 ⓦ www.maccosmetics.fr ⓛ 10.00–12.30, 14.00–18.30 Tues–Sat, closed Sun & Mon ⓝ Bus: 15

Mia Selection Organic clothes shop, stocking international, eco-friendly labels such as People Tree. ⓐ 23 rue de la Course ⓣ (05) 56 44 50 82 ⓛ 15.00–19.00 Mon, 10.00–13.00, 15.00–19.00 Tues–Sat, closed Sun ⓝ Tram: Place Paul Doumer

Papeterie de Malherbe North of place Gambetta, this old-fashioned shop sells a wide range of birthday and Christmas cards, more stylish and unusual than many you can find in France. ⓐ 5 rue Huguerie ⓣ (05) 56 48 16 65 ⓦ www.papeteriedemalherbe.com ⓛ 10.30–12.45, 13.45–19.00 Mon–Fri, 09.00–12.00, 14.30–19.00 Sat, closed Sun ⓝ Bus: 15

Pig and Rose Women and children are well catered for in this fashionable clothes boutique. ⓐ 130 cours de Verdun ⓣ (05) 56 44 61 39 ⓛ 10.30–13.00, 14.00–18.30 Tues–Sat, closed Sun & Mon ⓝ Bus: 4

TAKING A BREAK

10 Dowling Street £–££ ❶ British-themed coffeeshop, where you can stock up on baked beans and HP Sauce while enjoying their excellent snacks. A good wine selection also, to take away as well as consume on the premises. ⓐ 10 rue Sicard ⓣ (05) 56 01 20 90 ⓛ 08.00–20.00 Mon–Fri, 09.00–15.00 Sat, closed Sun ⓦ www.10-dowling-street.info ⓝ Tram: Place Paul Doumer

Nulle Part Ailleurs £–££ ❷ World Cup star and former Bordeaux player Christophe Dugarry owns this popular bar just behind place des Quinconces, which is a favourite haunt of many football fans. ⓐ 19 cours du Maréchal Foch ⓣ (05) 56 52 27 58 ⓛ 18.30–24.00 Mon–Sat, closed Sun ⓝ Tram: Quinconces

L'Orangerie £–££ ❸ Ah! A tea shop in the Jardin Public. Ice-cream coloured chairs outside for relaxing in summer, lots of plants inside to make you feel summery even if it's raining. Cream teas are available. ⓐ Jardin Public, cours de Verdun ⓣ (05) 56 48 24 41 ⓛ 08.00–19.30 ⓝ Tram: Jardin Public

La Vie en Rose ££ ❹ Fantastic tea shop that serves huge salads, quiches and sweet treats in a restful, feminine atmosphere. ⓐ 8 rue Sicard ⓣ (05) 56 48 03 44 ⓛ 09.00–19.00 Tues–Sat, closed Sun & Mon ⓝ Tram: Place Paul Doumer

AFTER DARK

RESTAURANTS
Chez Dupont £–££ ❺ Classic French bistro with a small number of tables outside. Good range of fish and meat dishes, and almost always a queue. ⓐ rue Notre Dame ⓣ (05) 56 81 49 59 ⓛ 12.00–14.00, 19.30–22.30 Tues–Sat, closed Sun & Mon ⓝ Tram: Place Paul Doumer

◖ *Relax and watch the world go by in one of the city's many cafés*

Le Boucher ££ ❻ Meat, meat and more meat, excellently prepared, very faithful crowd. ⓐ 35 rue Borie ❶ (05) 57 87 20 58 ❶ 19.30–23.00 Tues–Sat, closed Sun & Mon ⓝ Tram: Chartrons; bus: 29

Influence Wok ££ ❼ Pick and mix your fresh noodles and sauce. ⓐ 23 cours Portal ❶ (05) 57 59 12 17 ❶ 11.45–14.30 Mon, 11.45–14.30, 19.00–22.00 Tues–Sat, closed Sun ⓝ Tram: Place Paul Doumer

Le Sélénite ££ ❽ Contemporary styling and a good choice of fish and vegetarian dishes. On a quiet road at the far end of Chartrons, so not always as busy as it should be. ⓐ 6 pl. Paul Avisseau ❶ (05) 56 51 05 64 ⓦ www.leselenite.com ❶ 12.00–14.00, 19.30–23.00 ⓝ Tram: Chartrons; bus: 31

La Dame de Shanghai £££ ❾ Glamorous Asian-fusion restaurant housed in an old clipper boat, by the Bassins à Flot. Good bar downstairs that hosts DJ nights from Thursday to Saturday. ⓐ Bassins à Flot no. 1, quai Armand Lalande ❶ (05) 57 10 20 50 ⓦ www.damedeshanghai.com ❶ 20.00–23.00 ⓝ Tram: Bassins à Flot

L'Oiseau Bleu £££ ❿ Very romantic restaurant with excellent food. ⓐ 65 cours Portal ❶ (05) 56 81 09 39 ❶ 12.00–14.00, 20.00–23.00 ⓝ Tram: Place Paul Doumer; bus: 4, 31

PUBS, BARS & CLUBS

Le Blush Champagne bar and DJ nights give this Bacalan club sophistication. ⓐ Hangar 36, Bassins à Flot no. 1 ⓣ (05) 56 50 40 60 ⓛ 23.00–04.00 ⓝ Tram: Bassins à Flot

Buzuba A restaurant, bar and beer garden, where something different is always going on, from projecting films onto a big screen, to funk or rare groove DJ nights. ⓐ 1 rue Gironde, Bassins à Flot no. 1 ⓣ (05) 56 50 40 60 or 08 84 62 80 53 ⓛ 12.00–02.00 ⓝ Tram: Bassins à Flot

Cambridge Arms British pub that serves hearty fare from pies to fish and chips. ⓐ 27 rue Rode ⓣ (05) 56 51 19 22 ⓛ 10.30–02.00 ⓝ Tram: Chartrons ; bus: 31

Cave de la Corse The Jardin Public's best-kept secret – a classic neighbourhood off-licence, that sells wine to take away but also to drink on the premises, perched around old wine barrels surrounded by locals. Jazz nights sometimes, chess always. Closing time is flexible depending on how many people are in the bar. ⓐ 43 rue de la Course ⓣ (05) 56 52 62 57 ⓛ 10.30–13.00, 16.30–21.00, closed Sun & Mon ⓝ Tram: Place Paul Doumer

Molly Malone's Irish pub with great fish and chips and a good spot for watching big matches. ⓐ 83 quai des Chartrons ⓣ (05) 57 87 06 72 ⓦ www.molly-pub.com ⓛ 10.30–02.30 ⓝ Tram: Chartrons

The Right Bank, Bordeaux Lac, Bouliac & beyond

Until a few years ago, the Right Bank (known as La Bastide), was a no-go area, an industrial wasteland cut off from central Bordeaux by the wide river that flows between the two banks. But big investment – and most importantly the opening of the tram that crosses the Pont de Pierre – has reconnected this interesting area with the other side of the river bank. And the best views of the Bordeaux skyline, especially of place de la Bourse and the Miroir d'Eau at night, come from over here. Behind the Bastide lie some interesting suburbs, especially the pretty village of Bouliac. A little further afield, Bordeaux Lac might not live up to its leafy-sounding name, but there are very attractive open spaces, running tracks and, of course, the lake itself – as well as a large conference centre, a modern casino and a number of shopping centres.

SIGHTS & ATTRACTIONS

Bois de Bordeaux

This is the largest single green space in Bordeaux, located right alongside Bordeaux Lac. And this really is green space – parkland, rivers and woods interspersed with more formal arrangements such as children's playgrounds and sports tracks.
ⓐ av. de Pernon, Bordeaux Lac Ⓝ Bus: 31

Ⓓ *The new tramway crosses the old Pont de Pierre*

THE CITY

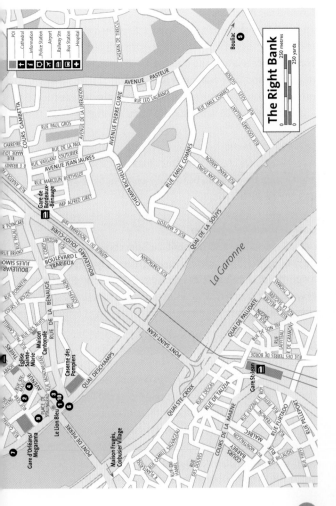

The Right Bank

0 — 250 metres
0 — 250 yards

KEY
☐ POI
☐ Cathedral
ℹ Information
☒ Police Station
✈ Airport
🚉 Railway Stn
🚌 Bus Station
✚ Hospital

La Garonne

Caserne des Pompiers

This striking 1950s building – loved and loathed in equal measure – is a firemen's depot that is the subject of several plans for preservation and improvement. Its architecture is modernist and 'ugly' – all corners and bright orange sidings – but compelling, and one of the landmarks that defines the Right Bank. ⓐ rue de la Benauge Ⓝ Tram: Stalingrad

Église Sainte-Marie

A very attractive church that dates back to the 1860s, with a lofty spire that is lit up beautifully every night. ⓐ av. Thiers Ⓝ Tram: Jardin Botanique

Gare d'Orléans/Megarama

Actually no longer a station, but a leisure complex by place de Stalingrad with a cinema, bowling alley, play area and a number of restaurants. ⓐ 7 quai des Queyries ⓣ 08 92 69 33 17 ⓦ www.megarama.fr ⓛ Varies according to film times, check ahead Ⓝ Tram: Stalingrad

Jardin Botanique

Opened in 2006, this Japanese-influenced botanical garden has several themed 'zones' and has become the focal point of the regeneration of the Right Bank. Among the many points of interest is the water garden, with its many plants and large stepping stones. There's also a section where local residents can grow their own vegetables, and a restaurant is opening soon. ⓐ quai des Queyries ⓛ 08.00–20.00 (summer); 08.00–18.30 (winter) Ⓝ Tram: Jardin Botanique

Jardins des Queyries

Leading directly off the river bank, this lung of green space provides fantastic views back over place de la Bourse and place des Quinconces. ⓐ quai des Queyries Ⓝ Tram: Jardin Botanique

BORDEAUX'S BRIDGES

There are three main bridges that cross the Garonne in Bordeaux – the Pont de Pierre built in the 1820s, and the Pont d'Aquitaine and the Pont Francois Mitterand, both built after 1960. There is also a steel railway bridge, built in the 1850s by Gustave Eiffel and used daily by hundreds of trains (including the high-speed TGV), and next to it a smaller road bridge. But really the only serious contender to link both banks is the Pont de Pierre – there are 6 km (nearly 4 miles) separating the Pont d'Aquitaine and the Pont de Pierre. This means that the Right Bank is still largely cut off from the Left and cycling or walking between the two means always crossing over at this one point. By car, there are always heavy traffic jams to negotiate (although the tramway that also uses the Pont de Pierre has helped ease traffic enormously). What all this means is that, for now, the regeneration of the Right Bank is very much contained by access to the bridge and its tramline. To improve this situation, a sixth bridge is planned to cross between Bacalan and the Bastide, with an estimated opening date of 2012. It is expected to be called Pont Lucien Faure, and has a projected budget of €120 million. Perhaps they'll get a bridging loan.

Le Lion Bleu, place de Stalingrad

One of the most striking sculptures in the city, this huge statue
of a blue lion was created by sculptor Xavier Veilhan, and has
proved very popular with local children, who often try to jump
off his giant paws. ⓐ pl. de Stalingrad ⓝ Tram: Stalingrad

Maison Cantonale

A striking art nouveau building dating from 1926 (it was intended
to be built a decade earlier, but World War I got in the way). Today
it houses a library, the local mayor's office and a police station.
ⓐ 42 rue des Nuits ⓝ Tram: Jardin Botanique

Maison Le Corbusier

This run-down but interesting road is one of Le Corbusier's
social housing projects, constructed in 1927, where he took the
same principles of industrial design, simple geometric spaces
and clean aesthetics and applied them to low-cost housing.
They haven't been kept particularly smart, but one is open
as a museum. Die-hard architecture fans will appreciate
this place the most. ⓐ 4 rue Le Corbusier, 33600 Pessac
ⓣ (05) 56 36 56 46 ⓛ 14.00–18.00 Wed–Fri, 14.00–18.30
Sat & Sun, closed Mon & Tues

Péniche Burdigala

Several boat trips are available up and down the river, from Pont
de Pierre, including tours of the five bridges of Bordeaux, or simply
steaming up and down the quays. Particularly beautiful at sunset.
ⓐ Pont de Pierre ⓣ (06) 07 19 75 86 ⓦ www.evolutiongaronne.com
ⓛ Phone to arrange a trip ⓝ Bus: Stalingrad

◔ *Take a boat trip for a riverside perspective of the city*

Piscine Galin

Public swimming pool that has a retractable roof for summer time. ⓐ 3 rue Galin ⓣ (05) 56 86 25 01 ⓛ 12.00–14.00, 17.00–19.00 Mon, Tues & Thur, 10.00–12.00, 15.00–20.00 Wed, 09.00–13.00 Sat & Sun, closed Fri ⓝ Tram: Thiers Benauge

Pont de Pierre

The oldest bridge that crosses the Garonne from place de Stalingrad to place Bir Hakeim, built in 1822. Its elegant arches

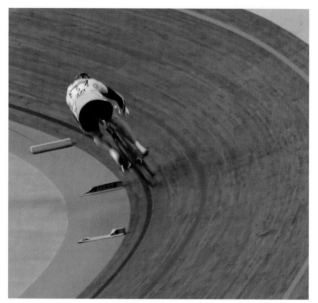

⬤ *Practice sessions at the Vélodrome*

and entire 490 metres (1,608 ft) are lit by traditional lamps and larger floodlights when night falls. Tram: Stalingrad or Port de Bourgogne

Vélodrome du Lac

Cycling competitions are held at this excellent track on a regular basis, but there is plenty of opportunity to use it for leisure cycling. ⓐ cours Jules Ladoumègue ⓣ (05) 56 43 16 05 ⓛ Varies according to event ⓝ Bus: 31

CULTURE

La Winery

About 20 minutes' drive from central Bordeaux, a newly opened winery with restaurant, tasting bar, concerts, large shop selling wines from around the world, and the chance to discover your 'wine horoscope'. ⓐ Rond-point des Vendangeurs, Départementale 1, 33460 Arsac-en-Médoc ⓣ (05) 56 39 04 90 ⓦ www.la-winery.fr ⓛ 11.00–20.00 Tues–Sun, closed Mon ⓝ Train: Gare St-Jean to Margaux, then ten minutes by car

RETAIL THERAPY

Boutique Bernard Magrez Château Pape Clément's wine shop, located just outside the château in the outlying suburb of Pessac. There are plans for a tasting school and restaurant on the premises, and the whole place is very glamorous. ⓐ Château Pape Clément, 216 av. du Docteur Nancel Penard, 33600 Pessac ⓣ (05) 57 26 43 04 ⓛ 11.00–18.00 Mon–Sat, closed Sun ⓝ Bus: 46, 47, 48

TAKING A BREAK

Délices et Café – Bordeaux Bastide £ ❶ Good spot for
breakfast or a snack lunch, with a wide range of herbal teas
and always at least two different *plats du jour* (dishes of
the day) on offer. ⓐ pl. de Stalingrad ❶ (05) 56 52 19 71
❶ 08.30–19.30 Mon–Fri, 10.00–19.30 Sat, closed Sun
Ⓝ Tram: Stalingrad

Les Temps Modernes £–££ ❷ Close to the Megarama cinema,
this cheerful café/bistro offers non-stop service, with larger
lunches and dinners served at midday and in the evenings.
ⓐ 27 rue Sainte-Marie ❶ (05) 56 40 50 78 ❶ 07.00–23.00
Mon–Fri, closed Sat & Sun Ⓝ Tram: Stalingrad

Brasserie L'Escale ££ ❸ Relaxed bistro for teas, coffees,
beers or something more substantial. Well located opposite
the Blue Lion. ⓐ 6 pl. de Stalingrad ❶ (05) 56 86 72 45
❶ 12.00–20.00 Mon–Sat, closed Sun Ⓝ Tram: Stalingrad

AFTER DARK

RESTAURANTS
La Mama £–££ ❹ Great pizza restaurant in a striking
building. The pizzas have thin, crispy bases, fresh toppings
and arrive fresh from a wood-fired oven. ⓐ 1 rue Sainte-Marie
❶ (05) 57 54 02 19 ❶ 12.00–14.00, 19.00–23.00 Mon–Sat,
closed Sun Ⓝ Tram: Stalingrad

Café de L'Espérance ££ ❺ Set in the pretty village of Bouliac, right by the Saint James Hotel, this is an upmarket bistro. The relaxed atmosphere is enhanced with great meat dishes and a groaningly good dessert trolley. ⓐ 33 rue de l'Esplanade ⓣ (05) 56 20 52 16 ⓛ 12.00–14.00, 19.00–23.00 Mon–Sat, closed Sun ⓝ Bus: 7

Café du Port ££ ❻ Large dining room overlooking the Garonne, with wooden tables, green plants and 1930s posters around the walls. Good range of seafood and gourmet meat dishes. ⓐ 1 quai Deschamps ⓣ (05) 56 77 81 18 ⓛ 12.00–14.00, 19.00–23.00 Mon–Sat, closed Sun ⓝ Tram: Stalingrad

L'Estacade ££ ❼ Restaurant on wooden stilts with one of the best views in town – directly back over the river to the Miroir d'Eau and place de la Bourse. Seafood is particularly good here, but the food takes second place to the setting. Excellent wine list. ⓐ quai des Queyries ⓣ (05) 57 54 02 50 ⓛ 12.30–14.30, 19.30–23.00 Mon–Sat, closed Sun ⓦ www.lestacade.com ⓝ Tram: Stalingrad

La Petite Gironde ££ ❽ Regular jazz and live music nights make this restaurant particularly appealing. ⓐ 75 quai des Queyries ⓣ (05) 57 80 33 31 ⓛ 12.00–14.00, 19.00–23.00 Mon–Fri, 19.00–23.00 Sat, 12.00–14.00 Sun ⓝ Tram: Stalingrad

Royal Bastide ££ ❾ One of the few Chinese restaurants on the Right Bank. ⓐ 7 quai des Queyries ⓣ (05) 56 86 88 99 ⓛ 12.00–14.00, 19.30–22.30 ⓝ Tram: Stalingrad

Le Wasabi Café ££ Japanese restaurant with excellent range of super-fresh sushi. ⓐ 3 pl. de Stalingrad ⓣ (05) 56 32 28 44 ⓛ 12.00–14.00, 20.00–22.30 Mon–Sat, closed Sun ⓝ Tram: Stalingrad

La Cape £££ Located in the residential suburb of Cenon, this is a Michelin-starred restaurant and a real find. The colourful decoration and artistically displayed food make this a sensory overload at times, but the meals are certainly memorable. ⓐ 9 allée de la Morlette, 33150 Cenon ⓣ (05) 57 80 24 25 ⓛ 12.00–14.00, 20.00–22.00 ⓝ Tram: Cenon

Le Château du Prince Noir (Restaurant Jean Marie Amat) £££ The latest addition to Bordeaux's restaurant scene, from renowned chef Jean Marie Amat. Expect a beautifully crafted and very fresh, seasonal menu from one of the region's most interesting characters. ⓐ 26 rue Raymond Lis, Lormont ⓣ (05) 56 06 12 52 ⓛ 12.00–14.00, 19.00–22.30 Tues–Fri, 19.30–23.00 Sat, closed Sun & Mon ⓝ Tram: Lormont Les Lauriers (terminus); bus: 66 (to Lormont Bas)

PUBS, BARS & CLUBS

Central Pub English-style pub with good range of beers and snacks – and the great advantage of continual service, unlike many places in Bordeaux. Gets lively later. ⓐ 7 quai des Queyries ⓣ (05) 57 80 38 00 ⓛ 12.00–02.00 ⓝ Tram: Stalingrad

Chez Alriq Coffees and teas are equally as good as the beers and wines at this relaxed *guingette* (riverside cafe). There are works

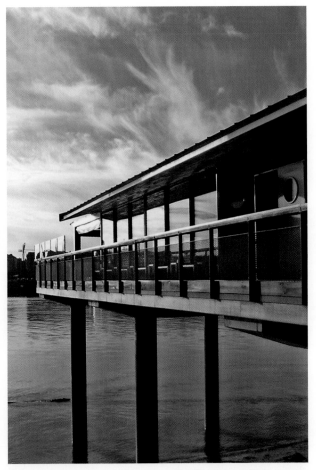

⬣ *L'Estacade has a prime location on the banks of the Garonne River*

planned, so although opening times below are just for summer, from 2009 this should be open year-round. ⓐ Port Bastide, quai des Queyries ⓣ (05) 56 86 58 49 ⓛ 20.00–22.00 Tues–Sun, closed Mon (summer) ⓝ Tram: Stalingrad

L'Eclypse Large club with a slightly older clientele, often with theme evenings. Can hold up to 1,000 clubbers, so any visiting DJs get a good reception. Located on the outskirts of the Bastide, on the road out to Bouliac. ⓐ 6 rue Jean Dupas, quai de la Souys ⓣ (05) 56 86 64 31 ⓦ www.eclypse-bordeaux.com ⓛ 22.00–04.00 Fri & Sat, closed Sun–Thur. Admission charge

Krakatoa Small, crowded and atmospheric concert venue where the likes of Kaiser Chiefs and Air have played. Concerts finish at midnight. ⓐ 3 av. Victor Hugo, Mérignac Arlac ⓣ (05) 56 24 34 29 ⓝ Tram: Mérignac Centre; bus: 50. Admission charge

Modern'Bar Smart bar with plenty of mirrors and polished brass. Good choice of beers. ⓐ 18 av. Thiers ⓣ (05) 56 86 35 55 ⓛ 11.00–14.00, 18.00–22.00 ⓝ Tram: Stalingrad

▶ *The vineyards of St Emillion*

Coastal resorts: Arcachon, Pyla & Cap Ferret

Just under an hour (or significantly more if caught in summer traffic) away from Bordeaux is the Atlantic Coast and the popular resorts of Arcachon, Pyla and Cap Ferret. Moving further up the coast there are a number of very good beaches, and even some large inland lakes that offer great water sports opportunities. Moving south of Arcachon, towards (eventually) Biarritz and the Spanish border, there are some fun surf resorts such as Mimizan. Wherever you choose to explore, the whole coast is a mixture of pine trees, beaches and sand dunes, and there are well-developed cycle and jogging paths that line the entire coastline.

● *Aerial view of Arcachon*

GETTING THERE

From the Gare St-Jean (see page 48), there are at least three return train services every day to Arcachon, and more in July and August.

To drive to Arcachon, take the A63 motorway from Bordeaux, then the A660 to Arcachon. For Le Porge take exit 23 off the A63 motorway by Marcheprime, then follow signs to Le Temple and Le Porge. For Pyla, take A63 motorway from Bordeaux. Then take the A660 towards Arcachon, the N250 and finally the D259 signposted Pyla.

There is a bus service from Archacon to Pyla, for details of which phone ☎ (05) 56 54 63 14. CITRAM Aquitaine also runs bus services in this region – phone ☎ (05) 56 70 17 27 for details.

SIGHTS & ATTRACTIONS

Dune de Pyla

Europe's highest sand dune stands at 105 metres (344 feet) tall. It overlooks the Arcachon Bassin (a sheltered inland bay), about 5 km (3 miles) from Arcachon town. From the top, you get great views over the bay to Cap Ferret on the far side. The dune in total is 2,500 metres (8,202 feet) long and 500 metres (1,640 feet) wide, and its slope is between 30° and 40° on the east side, and between 5° and 20° on the west. But don't worry; someone has kindly put a staircase in the side of the dune for climbing up to the top, from where you can walk for miles, admiring the view of boats in the bay. To get back down again, nothing beats running as fast as you can... Ⓦ www.dune-pyla.com

L'Île aux Oiseaux

A small island off the coast of Cap Ferret that takes its name from the large number of herons, geese and moorhens that live on and around it. There are also around 40 oyster farmer huts on the island, two of which are particularly famous for being suspended on poles (the famous *cabanes tchanquées*, a term that comes from the Gascon word for stilt). One of these huts is over a hundred years old (it's not open for visitors unfortunately, but makes for a very attractive photograph).

Lège Cap Ferret

Cap Ferret (or 'Ferret' as the locals call it) is *the* upmarket holiday spot of choice for the smart Bordelais. The whole place is a narrow strip of sand and land that extends 19 km (12 miles), and in summer,

🔺 *The vast expanse of sand at Dune de Pyla*

châteaux owners and wine merchants decamp here en masse. Among the attractions are a beautiful lighthouse, a beach on 'The Point' (La Pointe) that is located where the sheltered bay turns into the Atlantic Ocean, causing waves that get a lot bigger and more dramatic. There are also lots of great restaurants, and a number of chic clothes and food shops. It's possible to get to Cap Ferret by road or by boat from Arcachon. Just be warned that in summer time, the single road that leads to the Cap can get very over-crowded – you're best to leave either very early in the morning, or very late at night. ⓐ Lège Cap Ferret Tourist Office, 1 av. du Général de Gaulle, 33950 Lège Cap Ferret ⓣ (05) 56 03 94 49 ⓦ www.lege-capferret.com

The Médoc Lakes

There are three main lakes further up the coast from Cap Ferret and Le Porge towards the mouth of the estuary: Lac de Lacanau, Lac de Carcans and Lac d'Hourtin. All three are large and shallow, making for a safe environment for learning windsurfing or sailing. Inevitably this makes them very popular with families. All of the lakes, particularly Lacanau, are really unspoilt. Lac de Lacanau is lined with pine trees and has some lovely beaches. There are places to hire boats to sail around and investigate the coves and hidden bays. If you go right up to the Pointe du Verdon, you're at the far end of the Médoc where there are sailing clubs, mountain bike circuits and plenty of walking routes. ⓐ Halte Nautique de Lacanau Ville ① (05) 56 03 83 03

Oyster farmers

All over the Bassin you'll find oyster farmers, oyster huts, oyster festivals – these are particularly prevalent in Gujan-Mestras, Jacquets, Piraillan and l'Herbe. It's always worth driving into these villages, because you'll regularly run into an *ostréiculteur* who is happy to talk about the oysters, show you how to open them correctly, match them with wine – and even, if you're very lucky, to organise a special trip out on a boat to the farms.

Le Porge

A beach on the Atlantic coast, higher up than Cap Ferret but only 45 minutes from Bordeaux, with a long stretch of sand, lots of water sports and good spots for picnicking. It's wilder and more romantic than the perfectly manicured Arcachon beaches, and makes a great spot for walking and sand-castle building.

OYSTERS

Oyster parks cover huge areas around the Bassin, and there are over 350 individual businesses and farmers. All over the coastline, you'll find roadside stalls selling freshly shucked oysters. Most are sold direct from producers who have been up since dawn hauling them out of their beds. Arcachon oysters generally cost less than €5 for a dozen, and are more delicate than the colder-water oysters from Normandy, less salty than many from the Mediterranean. As they are farmed oysters, they are available year round – the old adage that you can only eat oysters in a month with an 'R' in it doesn't hold true here. But whatever the month, the best way of serving them is with a squeeze of lemon, a few lightly vinegared shallots, and of course a glass of white wine. Another typical serving suggestion of the southwest is with a spicy chitterling sausage on the side.

ⓐ Tourist office, 3 pl. St Seurin, 33680 Le Porge ⓣ (05) 56 26 54 34 ⓦ www.leporge.fr

CULTURE

La Chapelle de la Villa Algérienne

A beautiful chapel located at the far end of the beach in the pretty oyster village of l'Herbe. It was once attached to the grand Villa Algérienne (now largely destroyed, although small parts of the façade remain). ⓐ route du Cap Ferret, 33950 l'Herbe

Ets Charbonnier

Boat hire, but also scuba diving and fishing trips are available here. The same agency also rents out bikes for exploring the many bike paths that line the Cap. ⓐ 51 av. de l'Océan, 33970 Cap Ferret ⓣ (05) 56 60 61 87 ⓦ www.etscharbonnier.fr

Le Phare de Cap Ferret (The Lighthouse)

From the top of this 53-metre-high (174 ft) lighthouse, the view really is spectacular. Photography exhibitions are often held on the lower floors. ⓛ 10.00–19.30. Admission charge

RETAIL THERAPY

Antic Art & Déco Great place for browsing for gift ideas, or beautiful things for your house – a mix of antique and modern furniture, plus lamps and even sweets. ⓐ 75 route de Bordeaux, Petit-Piquey, 33950 Lège Cap Ferret ⓣ (05) 56 60 91 02 ⓦ www.anticartdeco.com ⓛ 10.00–18.00 Tues–Sat, closed Sun & Mon

TAKING A BREAK

La Cabane d'Edouard £ You just can't leave Cap Ferret without stopping at an oyster-tasting hut, and this is one of the best. ⓐ Port de Claouey, Cabanes 1 & 3, 33950 Lège Cap Ferret ⓣ (05) 57 70 30 44 ⓛ Varies depending on season and tide conditions; phone to check

ⓓ *Fishing boat moored beside an oyster farm in Arcachon Bay*

Café de la Plage £–££ The same building houses restaurant Chez Pierre, and both make the most of their excellent location with a large terrace. The atmosphere is relaxed and chic. As you'd expect, good seafood – but excellent breakfasts also. ⓐ 1 blvd Veyrier Montagnères, Arcachon ⓣ (05) 56 22 52 94 ⓦ http://cafedelaplage.com ⓛ 09.00–19.00

Eden Gourmands £–££ If you discover this place too early during your stay in Cap Ferret, you might be going back carrying a few extra pounds, thanks to the hand-made pâtisseries, chocolates and ice creams. ⓐ 64 route de Bordeaux, 33950 Lège Cap Ferret ⓣ (05) 56 60 51 38 ⓦ www.edengourmands-chez-patachou.com ⓛ 07.00–13.00, 15.30–20.00 (summer); 07.30–13.00, 15.30–19.00 (winter)

AFTER DARK

Le Mimbeau ££ Always popular bistro specialising in seafood (and excellent accompanying chips). Lovely terrace overlooking the ocean. ⓐ 52 blvd de la Plage, 33970 Lège Cap Ferret ⓣ (05) 57 70 39 92 ⓛ 12.00–14.00, 19.30–22.30

Chez Hortense ££–£££ The best known fish restaurant on the Bassin overlooks the water and has a very relaxed atmosphere. The food is wonderful, especially the speciality, *moules* (mussels). And don't just wait till after dark for this – the view over the Bassin makes lunchtimes particularly special. ⓐ av. du Semaphore, Lège Cap Ferret ⓣ (05) 56 60 62 56 ⓛ 12.00–14.00, 19.00–23.00 Wed–Mon, closed Tues

Le Chipiron ££–£££ There's a Spanish flavour at this popular restaurant located just by the port in Arcachon. ⓐ 69 blvd de Gal-Chanzy, Arcachon ⓣ (05) 57 52 00 33 ⓛ 12.00–14.00, 19.00–22.30

ACCOMMODATION

Hôtel de la Plage, Cap Ferret £–££ Simple and well located on the Atlantic beach side of Cap Ferret. ⓐ 1 av. des Marins, L'Herbe ⓣ (05) 56 60 50 15

La Pergola, Arcachon £–££ A guesthouse that offers excellent value in the middle of Arcachon. Not exactly imaginatively decorated rooms, but clean, many with terraces and views. ⓐ 40 cours Lamarque-de-Plaisance ⓣ (05) 56 83 07 89 ⓦ www.hotel-lapergola.net

Hôtel des Dunes ££ Renovated in 2006, this has a sauna, Wi-Fi and is located within easy reach of the village of Cap Ferret, as well as its beaches. ⓐ 119 av. de Bordeaux, 33970 Cap Ferret ⓣ (05) 56 60 61 81 ⓦ www.hoteldesdunes.com

Maison du Bassin, Cap Ferret ££–£££ This place is only open six months of the year, and books up far in advance, but it's wonderful. New England in feel, laid back but with real attention to detail in the rooms, with great restaurant and bar (with home-made rums). ⓐ 5 rue des Pionniers ⓣ (05) 56 60 60 63 ⓦ www.lamaisondubassin.com

The vineyards of the Saint Émilion region

If you don't want the beach, head out instead to the vineyards and the beautiful medieval town of Saint Émilion. This lies to the east of the city, about half an hour from Bordeaux towards the Dordogne Valley, and contains some of its most attractive landscapes, with gently undulating hills and miles of vineyards interspersed with small villages, woods and plenty of churches and historical monuments. It can be hard to get into some of the more prestigious wine properties such as Château Petrus or Château Cheval Blanc, but there are lots of winemakers who are only too happy to show you around and share a tasting – and make sure you include at least one whose barrels are stored in an underground cellar, dug out of the limestone hillsides (most of the buildings along the riverfront in Bordeaux centre, incidentally, were made from limestone taken out of quarries around Saint Émilion).

GETTING THERE

By train, from Bordeaux Gare St-Jean to Saint-Émilion Station, take the Bordeaux-Sarlat line (run by local train company TER). There are four trains (Bordeaux-Libourne-Sarlat) per day in each direction.

Take the N89 road from Bordeaux to Libourne and continue along until the Libourne Est-St Émilion exit on the D243 road.

SIGHTS & ATTRACTIONS

Castillon-la-Bataille
A smart but quiet town full of lovely 18th-century architecture and

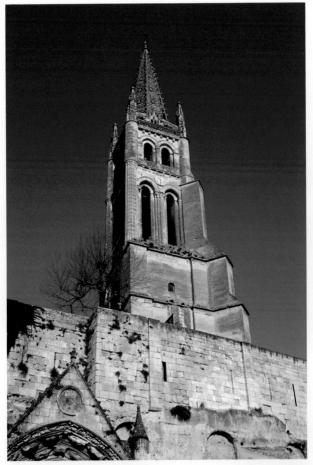

⬤ *The striking church spire in Saint Émilion*

a few upmarket shops (it's particularly good for foodies, as there are a number of well-stocked epiceries and delicatessens). Nice views also, as the town is right on the banks of the Dordogne River.

Cycling & walking paths

There are great cycling paths all over Bordeaux, and this one – going from Sauveterre-de-Guyenne, through Créon and back into Bordeaux – is one of the prettiest, allowing you to ride alongside vineyards for most of the way. ⓐ La Gare, blvd Victor-Hugo, 33670 Créon ⓣ (05) 57 34 30 95 ⓦ http://creonstationvelos.free.fr

Entre deux Mers

Entre deux Mers covers the large area to the south of the city, from the right bank of the Garonne, over Saint Émilion and the Dordogne. Some of the prettiest villages to look out for include Sauveterre-de-Guyenne, Branne and Monségur.

Libourne

This is a Bastide town with pretty quays and a central square, place Abel Surchamps, that was once fortified and still has elegant arcades. There are also some beautiful quays, where, in the 18th century, wine from Saint Émilion, Pomerol and Entre deux Mers was loaded onto flat-bottomed barges and sent off to northern France and further afield in Europe.

Pujols-sur-Dordogne

Village with status 'prettiest village in France'. Lots of flowers lining the streets, an attractive church and a square with good views over the Dordogne Valley.

UNESCO WORLD HERITAGE

Both Saint Émilion and Bordeaux are now UNESCO World Heritage Sites. This means that the World Heritage Committee considers them to possess a cultural pedigree of universal value. Their reason for classifying Saint Émilion is that it's 'an outstanding example of an historic vineyard landscape that has survived intact and in activity to the present day'. For Bordeaux, the committee commended the fact that, 'its urban form represents the success of philosophers who wanted to make towns into melting pots of humanism, universality and culture'.

Saint Émilion

The most tourist-friendly town in the Bordeaux region, this 8th-century medieval village has been a UNESCO World Heritage Site since 1999. It takes its name from a Breton monk who settled in a grotto in the forest that at the time covered the town's hill. A village grew up around him, as he fasted, prayed and generally performed miracles. You can still visit the original Émilion cave today, plus the many underground monuments that have grown up around his legend, most impressively the monolithic church and catacombs. Above ground, the buildings are carved out of the butter-coloured limestone that was the result of all these religious (and, later, practical) excavations. The town itself is based around two main squares – place du Clocher and place du Marché, and it's a great place for eating and shopping, and, of course, wine tasting.

CULTURE

Abbaye de Sauve Majeure

Eleventh-century Benedictine monastery, now in ruins but with the tower well preserved. You can walk to the top for fantastic views. **ⓐ** 2 rue de L'Abbaye, 33670 La Sauve-Majeure **ⓣ** (05) 56 23 01 55 **ⓛ** 10.00–18.00 Tues–Sun, closed Mon

Battle of Castillon re-enactment

On 17 July 1453, English forces were finally driven from Aquitaine after losing this historic battle in the Hundred Years' War. Every July and August, the thrashing of the English is re-enacted over a number of weekends. It's great fun to watch, with horses pounding over distant hills, a two-hour show performed on a massive stage and fireworks to end the night. **ⓐ** 5 allées de la République, 33150 Castillon la Bataille **ⓣ** (05) 57 40 1 4 53 **ⓦ** www.batailledecastillon.com

Musée Souterrain de la Poterie (Underground Pottery Museum)

There are over 6,000 exhibits here, with pottery ranging from over 20 centuries of local history. **ⓐ** Hospices de la Madeleine, 21 rue André Loiseau, 33300 Saint Émilion **ⓣ** (05) 57 24 60 93 **ⓦ** www.saint-emilion-museepoterie.fr **ⓛ** 10.00–19.00. Admission charge

Planète Bordeaux

A great place to come to learn about the history of winemaking. It's recently been updated and made far more interactive and fun, with a children's play area. Over 1,000 wines are available

to buy. ⓐ Maison des Bordeaux ⓐ RN 89, exit 5, 33750
Beychac et Cailleau ⓣ (05) 57 97 19 36 ⓕ (05) 57 97 19 37
ⓦ www.maisondesbordeaux.com ⓛ 10.00–19.00 (last
admission 18.00) May–Oct; 09.30–12.00, 14.00–17.30 Nov–Apr.
Admission charge

Tonnellerie du Monde

A fascinating opportunity to see wine barrels being made.
You'll get a whole new appreciation of the importance that wood
plays in ageing wine. ⓐ 8 route de Canteloup, 33750 Beychac
et Cailleau ⓣ (05) 56 72 82 00 ⓦ www.tonnelleriedumonde.fr
ⓛ By appointment only

RETAIL THERAPY

Comptoir des Vignobles Well-stocked wine shop in the heart
of the village, with lots of old vintages and English-speaking
staff. Not cheap, but a good place to browse for famous names.
ⓐ 1 rue des Girondins, 33300 Saint Émilion ⓣ (05) 57 24 61 10
ⓦ www.comptoir-des-vignobles.com ⓛ 10.00–19.00

Les Macarons de Saint Émilion The Harrods of macaroon emporia.
ⓐ rue Guadet, 33300 Saint Émilion ⓣ (05) 57 24 72 33
ⓛ 09.30–12.00, 14.30–18.00

La Ronde des Fromages The covered market in Libourne is worth
a visit for its fresh produce and two excellent cheese stands.
ⓐ Covered market, 33500 Libourne ⓣ (06) 78 92 26 26
ⓛ Every morning except Sun

TAKING A BREAK

Le Web Bar £ A stylish cybercafé with a nice line in comestibles.
ⓐ 37 rue Guadet ⓣ (05) 57 24 52 45 ⓦ www.saintemilionwebbar.com
ⓛ 11.00–21.00 Tues–Sat, closed Sun & Mon

Café Guingette ££ Outside tables along the river front in Libourne, with a good selection of salads and fish. Open summer only, and lunchtime only. ⓐ 13 quai du Général d'Amade, 33500 Libourne
ⓣ (05) 57 51 87 87 ⓛ 12.00–14.00 May–Aug

L'Envers du Décor ££ Very popular restaurant with excellent wine list and a sheltered courtyard out the back for sunny days.
ⓐ 11 rue du Clocher, 33300 Saint Émilion ⓣ (05) 57 74 48 31
ⓛ 12.00–14.00, 19.00–21.00

● *Laid-back café culture in Saint Émilion*

AFTER DARK

L'Atmosphère, St Germain du Puch ££ Jazz music, great menu, summery feel with greenery all over... really worth driving for (15 mins via the A631, N230, E70). ⓐ 99 Le Bourg, 33750 St Germain du Puch ⓣ (05) 58 24 52 34 ⓛ 12.00–14.30, 19.00–23.00

L'Essentiel ££ Very slick wine bar in Saint Émilion, where you can try big name châteaux by the glass. Plates of cheeses and hams are also available. ⓐ 6 rue Guadet, 33300 Saint Émilion ⓣ (05) 57 24 39 76 ⓦ www.essentiel-vin.com ⓛ 11.00–20.00

La Poudette ££ Seasonal produce and market finds dominate the menu at this lovely restaurant. ⓐ 1 Bernadigot, 33350 Pujols-sur-Dordogne ⓣ (05) 57 40 71 52 ⓦ www.la-poudette.com ⓛ 12.00–14.00, 19.30–23.00 Tues–Sun, closed Mon

La Maison du Fleuve ££–£££ This contemporary restaurant has a lovely terrace overlooking the Garonne River. ⓐ 20 Chemin Seguin, Port Neuf, 33360 Camblanes et Meynac ⓣ (05) 56 20 06 40 ⓦ www.maison-du-fleuve.com ⓛ 12.30–13.30, 19.30–21.30 Tues–Sat, 12.30–13.30 Sun, closed Mon

ACCOMMODATION

Château Hôtel Isabeau de Naujan ££ Recently-restored wine château that has some lovely rooms and a good restaurant. ⓐ Domaine de Naujan, 33420 Saint Vincent de Pertignas ⓣ (05) 57 55 14 33 ⓦ www.domaine-de-naujan.com

● *The Château de Sanse is one of the area's prettiest hotels*

Château du Petit Puch, St Germain du Puch £f Charming place
to stay where you can experience a genuine winemaking château.
The four rooms are located in one wing of the property.
ⓐ 33750 St Germain du Puch ⓣ (05) 57 24 52 36
ⓦ www.chateaupetitpuch.com

Château de Sanse £f Near to Castillon and St Foy La Grande,
this 18th-century château has been stylishly refurbished and
has good views from the restaurant over the surrounding
countryside. ⓐ 33350 Ste Radegonde ⓣ (05) 57 56 41 10
ⓕ (05) 57 56 41 29 ⓦ www.chateaudesanse.com

○ *The tramway is a relaxing and efficient way to get around the city*

PRACTICAL
information

Directory

GETTING THERE

By air

Bordeaux-Mérignac Airport (see page 48) is served by many airlines, including:

Aer Lingus 🕿 (01) 70 20 00 72 🌐 www.aerlingus.ie
Air France 🕿 08 20 82 08 20 🌐 www.airfrance.fr
BMI 🕿 (01) 41 91 87 04 🌐 www.flybmi.com
British Airways 🕿 08 25 82 54 00 🌐 www.britishairways.com
easyJet 🕿 08 25 08 25 08 🌐 www.easyjet.com

The flight time from London is approximately 75 minutes.

Many people are aware that air travel emits CO_2, which contributes to climate change. You may be interested in the possibility of lessening the environmental impact of your flight through Climate Care, which offsets your CO_2 by funding environmental projects around the world. Visit 🌐 www.climatecare.org for details.

Remember airports are working under conditions of heightened security at the moment, and you should always allow plenty of time for check-in. Baggage allowances may also change, so check with your airline in advance of flying.

By rail

The rail journey from London St Pancras International via Eurostar to Paris Gare du Nord, and then by TGV from Paris to Bordeaux should take about six hours in total (trains run regularly throughout the day).

Eurostar for cross-Channel trains ☎ 08705 186 186
ⓦ www.eurostar.com
SNCF for trains within France ☎ 08 92 35 35 35
ⓦ www.voyages-sncf.com
Thomas Cook European Rail Timetable ☎ (01733) 416 477
ⓦ www.thomascookpublishing.com

By road

From Calais, the A1 goes down to Bordeaux, and the car
journey should total around eight hours. For driving from
the UK via Calais – and thus via **Eurotunnel** (☎ 08705 353 535
ⓦ www.eurotunnel.com) you should make it down in one day,
with stops. From northern Spain, you should reach Bordeaux
in three hours.

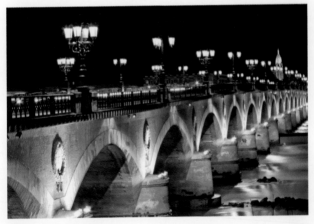

⏴ Pont de Pierre by night

Remember to bring both parts of your driving licence and to inform your insurance company before driving to France. You should carry a copy of your valid insurance certificate.

If you fancy making the trip by coach, **Eurolines** (ⓦ www.eurolines.com), Europe's largest coach operator, serves all of France and the rest of the Continent.

When you've arrived in the region, information on traffic is available on ⓣ (05) 61 12 77 77

By water

The nearest international ferry port is in Caen. Bordeaux is then a six-hour drive from Caen. Alternatively, you can take a ferry to Santander in Spain and drive up (about five hours drive time). **Brittany Ferries** ⓣ 08 25 82 88 28 ⓦ www.brittany-ferries.com **P&O Ferries** ⓣ 08705 980 333 ⓦ www.poferries.com

ENTRY FORMALITIES

EU citizens can travel to France without a visa. For USA, Canada, Australia, New Zealand, South Africa, visits of up to three months do not require a visa.

But for all entries, you do need an identity card with photograph, which really means your passport.

Residents of UK, Ireland and other EU countries may bring into France personal possessions and goods for personal use, provided they have been bought in the EU (and therefore no luggage that contains goods intended for sale as these would be subject to import taxes). For full regulations and definitions of 'reasonable amounts' visit ⓦ www.douane.gouv.fr

For taking animals to France, the same rules apply as with the rest of the EU (ie they need a European (EU) Pet Passport). All vets should have the relevant information and be able to get your animal ready for travelling with you.

MONEY

The currency of France is the euro (€). 1 euro = 100 cents (also called eurocents). Euros come in notes of €5, €10, €20, €50, €100, €200, €500. Coins are in denominations of €1 and €2, and in cents worth 1c, 2c, 5c, 10c, 20c and 50c. For current exchange rates, check Ⓦ www.travelex.com or Ⓦ www.oanda.com

ATM machines are plentiful in Bordeaux and are the easiest way to withdraw money while you're there. Traveller's cheques and foreign money can be cashed at most banks, bureaux de change and some hotels. You will need your passport as identification. Major international credit cards are accepted in most large stores and restaurants and in ATM machines.

HEALTH, SAFETY & CRIME

Drinking water is safe, and many public parks have drinking fountains (if not it is marked *Eau Non Potable*, or 'Water Not for Drinking'). There are plenty of hospitals and doctors, and medical facilities in Bordeaux are excellent.

No inoculations are necessary for travelling to France. If you have any queries, it's always worth asking your doctor before leaving, or reading the Department of Health advice in your home country. In the UK, info is on Ⓦ www.dh.gov.uk (in the Travel Advice section). It's always advisable to take a small first-aid kit with you, and keep it in the car if you are travelling around.

Pharmacies are easily found – look for the green crosses – and available throughout the city. One of the most convenient is **Pharmacie de la Bourse** (ⓐ 3 quai Richelieu ⓣ (05) 56 90 94 04 ⓛ 09.00–19.30 Mon–Fri, 09.00–19.30 Sat, closed Sun).

A European Health Insurance Card (EHIC; ⓦ www.ehiccard.org) entitles you to reduced-cost, sometimes free, medical treatment that becomes necessary while you're in a European Economic Area (EEA) country or Switzerland. The EHIC has replaced the old E111.

OPENING HOURS

Banks ⓛ 09.00–12.30, 14.00–17.00 Mon–Fri, larger branches also 09.00–12.00 Sat

Shops ⓛ 09.30 or 10.00–12.30, 14.00–19.00 Mon–Sat

Pharmacies ⓛ 08.30 or 09.00–12.00, 14.00–19.00 Mon–Sat, larger branches also 09.00–12.30 Sun

Restaurants ⓛ 12.00–14.00, 19.00–22.30 although some are closed Mondays

Many museums are closed on Mondays; many vineyards close on Sundays (and some also on Saturdays, so call ahead).

TOILETS

There are public toilets at several places in the city centre and most are clean and well kept – there are several new ones along the quays, and at key points through the city centre such as place Paul Doumer in Chartrons. There are occasionally separate ones for men and women, and most will have an entrance fee. The airport and the train station both have good public toilets, and most museums are also a good bet for clean, attractive facilities.

There are very few old-style 'hole in the ground' French toilets left in the city, and almost all are now modern European style.

CHILDREN

Bordeaux, despite its reputation for being reserved, is very child-friendly, and small children will be welcomed in almost all hotels, cafés and restaurants. Many of them provide not only high chairs but also colouring pencils and paper to keep little ones entertained. Pharmacies will sell nappies, baby food, suntan lotion and everything you might need.

On top of all that, the city has a number of fabulous attractions. For example, at **Cap Sciences** (ⓐ Hangar 20 quai Bacalan ① (05) 56 01 07 07 ⓦ www.cap-sciences.net), on Wednesdays, Saturdays and Sundays between June and January, there are short 'Petit Explorateur' ('Little Explorer') sessions for three- to six-year-olds, and separate ones for the five to eleven age group. The Miroir d'Eau (see page 62) is a haven for young children,

🔴 The surprising Miroir d'Eau keeps everyone amused

especially in hot weather, where they can be kept amused for hours running in and out of the jets of water, or paddling when it turns into a still, reflective (and very shallow) lake. If your little ones need to expend some energy, Ludothèque, a large play area located by the Jardin Botanique on the Right Bank is ideal, with its massive indoor and outdoor amusements. There are good playgrounds all over the city, and two are in the Jardin Public (see page 78). Older teenagers will love the **Skate Park** on quai des Chartrons (ⓐ 37 allée Jean Giono ⓣ (05) 56 67 94 25), which also provides games for all ages, and multimedia activities for over-sevens.

COMMUNICATIONS
Internet
Bordeaux is an extensively wired (or, rather, wireless) city. Many of the bars and cafés around place des Chartrons are all Wi-Fi'd up, and there are several internet cafés on rue Notre Dame, and lots more off place Gambetta on rue du Palais Gallien.

Phone
Card-operated public phone boxes are available across Bordeaux, and international calls can be made from them. You have to buy a *telecarte* (phonecard) at a *tabac* (newsagent's/cigarette shop). **Directory Enquires** ⓣ 118712 from any phone

Post
Postal services are very reliable across France. Post offices sell telephone cards, and usually have photocopiers or a fax machine available for public use. Most have coin operated machines for

TELEPHONING BORDEAUX

The area code for southwest France is 05, followed by a number which is always eight digits in length. When dialling from anywhere in France, use all eight digits, including the 05.

To call Bordeaux numbers from outside of France, dial your own international prefix (00 in most countries) then 33 for France, then drop the initial 0 of the 05.

TELEPHONING ABROAD

To call abroad from France, dial 00 for an international connection, then your own country code (44 for the UK, 353 Republic of Ireland, 1 USA or Canada, 61 Australia, 64 New Zealand, 27 South Africa), then the area code leaving out the intial 0.

buying stamps and weighing packages if you don't want to wait in line (many French people do their banking through the post office, so queues can be long).

Post boxes are yellow and easy to spot. Stamps can be bought either from the post office or from a *tabac* (newsagent's/cigarette shop).

The two main post offices in Bordeaux are:

La Poste Bordeaux Saintonge ⓐ 2 rue Saintonge ⓣ (05) 56 99 30 80 ⏱ 08.30–18.00 Mon–Fri, 08.30–12.00 Sat, closed Sun

La Poste Bordeaux Tourny ⓐ 29 allées de Tourny ⓣ (05) 56 00 88 70 ⏱ 09.00–18.00 Mon–Thur, 09.00–12.00 Fri, 09.00–12.00, 14.00–18.00 Sat, closed Sun

ELECTRICITY

France runs on 220 volts with two-pin plugs. British appliances will need an adaptor, easily obtained at any electrical or hardware store, or at the airport. US and other equipment designed for 110 volts will need a transformer (*transformateur*).

TRAVELLERS WITH DISABILITIES

Bordeaux airport and train stations have good access points for travellers who need extra assistance, and there are lifts in most of the larger hotels. The trams have good access for people with disabilities. However, buses tend to be ill-equipped, and there are many hotels which do not have bathrooms and bedrooms that are easily adapted to wheelchairs. Useful organisations for information and advice include:

RADAR The principal UK forum and pressure group for people with disabilities. ⓐ 12 City Forum, 250 City Road, London EC1V 8AF ⓣ (020) 7250 3222 ⓦ www.radar.org.uk

SATH (Society for Accessible Travel & Hospitality) Advises US-based travellers with disabilities. ⓐ 347 Fifth Ave, Suite 610, New York NY 10016 ⓣ 212 447 7284 ⓦ www.sath.org ⓔ sathtravel@aol.com

Association des Paralyses en France ⓐ Délégation Départementale des Alpes Maritimes, 3 avenue Antoine Véran, Nice ⓣ (04) 92 07 98 00 ⓦ www.apf.asso.fr ⓔ apf.dd06@wanadoo.fr

TOURIST INFORMATION

To reach any tourist board in France, dial 3264 and clearly say the name of the town or city you are interested in. You will be put through automatically to the correct tourist office. Calls cost 34 cents per minute.

Maison de La France (French Tourist Board) The UK branch can offer plenty of info before you leave. ⓐ 178 Piccadilly, London W1J 9AL ⓣ 09068 244 123 (calls cost 60p per min) ⓦ www.franceguide.com

Bordeaux Tourist Office ⓐ 12 cours du 30 juillet, 33000 Bordeaux ⓣ (05) 56 00 66 00 ⓦ www.bordeaux-tourisme.com ⓛ 09.00–19.30 Mon–Sat, 09.30–18.30 Sun, July & Aug; 09.00–19.00 Mon–Sat, 09.30–18.30 Sun, Sept–June

Saint Émilion Tourist Office ⓐ pl. des Créneaux, Saint Émilion ⓣ (05) 57 55 28 28 ⓛ opening hours vary with the season ⓦ www.saint-emilion-tourisme.com

Maison du Tourisme et du Vin de Pauillac ⓐ La Verrerie, Pauillac ⓣ (05) 56 59 03 08 ⓛ 09.30–12.30, 14.00–18.00 Mon–Sat, 10.30–12.00, 15.00–17.30 Sun

BACKGROUND READING

Bordeaux People, Power and Politics by Stephen Brook. A good overview of Bordeaux's wine industry.

Resistance and Betrayal: The Death and Life of Jean Moulin, the Greatest Hero of the French Resistance by Patrick Marnham. A compelling study of a complex, hugely brave man, and a history of the activities of the Resistance in general.

Noble Rot: A Bordeaux Wine Revolution by William Echikson. Salacious and fascinating insight into the petty politics of the wine world.

PRACTICAL INFORMATION

Emergencies

The following are emergency freephone numbers:

Ambulance ❶ 15

Fire ❶ 18

Police ❶ 17

All emergency services from a mobile phone ❶ 112

MEDICAL SERVICES

French medical facilities are excellent. Visitors from the UK require a European Health Insurance Card (EHIC); this will not cover all expenses, and only guarantees emergency treatment. Travel insurance for health and possessions is advised. All non-EU travellers should arrange adequate insurance.

EMERGENCY PHRASES

Help!   Au secours!   *Oh suhcoor!*

Call the police/fire service/ambulance!
Appelez la police/les pompiers/une ambulance!
Appeley lah police/leh pompee-eh/oon ambulance!

I am allergic to nuts/dairy
Je suis allergique aux cacahuètes/produits laitiers
Zher swee alairjeek o kakawet/prodwee laytyay

Emergency doctors
SOS Médecins ☎ (05) 56 44 74 74 or (05) 56 99 77 77

Emergency dentist
Médico-Dentaire Health Centre @ 45 rue Vital Charles
☎ (05) 56 44 93 78 🕐 09.00–19.00 Mon–Fri, 09.00–12.00 Sat,
closed Sun

Hospitals
Saint-André Hospital @ 1 rue Jean Burguet ☎ (05) 56 79 56 79
Children's Hospital (Hôpital des Enfants) @ Groupe Hospitalier
Pellegrin ☎ (05) 56 79 56 79

POLICE
Lost property @ 99 rue Abbé de l'Épée ☎ (05) 56 44 20 18
🕐 08.30–16.30 Mon–Fri, closed Sat & Sun
Police Office (main police headquarters) @ 29 rue Castéja
☎ (05) 56 99 77 77

EMBASSIES & CONSULATES
British Consulate @ 353 blvd de Président Wilson,
33000 Bordeaux ☎ (05) 57 22 21 10
Canadian Consulate @ 10 rue Jules de Rességuier, Toulouse
☎ (05) 61 52 19 06 🕐 09.00–12.00 Mon–Fri, closed Sat & Sun
Spanish Consulate @ 16 rue Sainte Anne, Toulouse ☎ (05) 34 31 96 60
🕐 09.00–14.00 Mon–Fri, closed Sat & Sun
US Consulate General @ 10 pl. de la Bourse ☎ (05) 56 48 63 80
🕐 09.00–14.00 Mon–Fri, closed Sat & Sun

Send your thoughts to
books@thomascook.com

- Found a great bar, club, shop or must-see sight that we don't feature?
- Like to tip us off about any information that needs a little updating?
- Want to tell us what you love about this handy little guidebook and more importantly how we can make it even handier?

Then here's your chance to tell all! Send us ideas, discoveries and recommendations today and then look out for your valuable input in the next edition of this title.

Email the above address (stating the title) or write to:
CitySpots Project Editor, Thomas Cook Publishing, PO Box 227, Coningsby Road, Peterborough PE3 8SB, UK.

ACKNOWLEDGEMENTS

Editorial/project management: Lisa Plumridge with Laetitia Clapton
Copy editor: Paul Hines
Layout/DTP: Alison Rayner
Proofreader: Wendy Janes

The publishers would like to thank the Bordeaux Tourist Office and following individuals and organisations for supplying their copyright photographs for this book: Christian Baeur/SXC.hu, page 24; Douglas Barry, page 86; BigStockPhoto.com (Henri Frontier, pages 57, 98 & 106–7; Rafael Laguillo, pages 1, 40–1 & 115); Château de Sanse, page 126; Comite Regional du Tourisme de Aquitaine/Jean-Jacques Brochard, pages 111, 119 & 124; Dreamstime.com (Hubert Coia, page 81; Claude Coquilleau, pages 33, 129 & 133; Henri Frontier, page 34; Duncan Gilbert, page 47); Fotolia.com (Phil B, pages 9 & 65; Jean-Luc Le Cuillier, page 15; Antoine Declerck, page 127; Marie Emeri, page 19; Gelinaud, page 97; Hubert, pages 43, 45 & 59; Jacques Palut, pages 28, 75 & 103; stockfoto, page 91); Mike Hanson, page 70; iStockphoto.com (John Cave, page 105; Mike Dabell, page 23; Bart De Meuter, page 7; Gregory Van Raalte, pages 30–1); Zachary Mastoon, page 49; Martha Richards, page 21; Katie Reeder, page 68; Sources de Caudalie, page 39; Frederico Spengler, page 11; untipografico, page 72